USING THE BIBLE IN PRACTICAL THEOLOGY

In this groundbreaking book Zoë Bennett brilliantly sketches the public theology of John Ruskin and skilfully uses it to illuminate practical theology and biblical hermeneutics. It is an outstanding contribution, not only to public theology but also to theology more generally. Calling on a wide array of interpretative skills, she illuminates a subject of pressing concern in a readable and compelling manner and demonstrates the value of historical study for the development of critical reflection. The study of John Ruskin, the Bible and theology will never look the same again.

Christopher Rowland, Queens College, Oxford, UK

Exploring how the Bible may be appropriately used in practical and public theology, this book looks at types of modern practical theology with specific emphasis on the use of the Bible. Bennett juxtaposes the diversity of modern practical theology with the work of leading nineteenth-century public 'theologian', John Ruskin, and then assesses the contribution of this analysis to some modern issues of public importance in which the Bible is used. The final chapter offers a framework for a biblically informed critical practical theology which draws on the writer's experience and invites the readers to engage their own.

Explorations in Practical, Pastoral and Empirical Theology

Series Editors

Leslie J. Francis, University of Warwick, UK
Jeff Astley, North of England Institute for Christian Education, UK
Martyn Percy, Ripon College Cuddesdon and The Oxford
Ministry Course, Oxford, UK

Theological reflection on the church's practice is now recognized as a significant element in theological studies in the academy and seminary. Ashgate's series in practical, pastoral and empirical theology seeks to foster this resurgence of interest and encourage new developments in practical and applied aspects of theology worldwide. This timely series draws together a wide range of disciplinary approaches and empirical studies to embrace contemporary developments including: the expansion of research in empirical theology, psychological theology, ministry studies, public theology, Christian education and faith development; key issues of contemporary society such as health, ethics and the environment; and more traditional areas of concern such as pastoral care and counselling.

Other titles in the series include:

Exploring Ordinary Theology
Everyday Christian Believing and the Church
Edited by Jeff Astley and Leslie J. Francis

Asylum-Seeking, Migration and Church
Susanna Snyder

How Survivors of Abuse Relate to God
The Authentic Spirituality of the Annihilated Soul
Susan Shooter

Ordinary Christology
Who Do You Say I Am? Answers From The Pews
Ann Christie

The Ecclesial Canopy
Faith, Hope, Charity
Martyn Percy

Using the Bible in Practical Theology
Historical and Contemporary Perspectives

ZOË BENNETT
Cambridge Theological Federation with Anglia Ruskin University, UK

ASHGATE

Published by
Ashgate Publishing Limited
Wey Court East
Union Road
Farnham
Surrey, GU9 7PT
England

Ashgate Publishing Company
110 Cherry Street
Suite 3-1
Burlington, VT 05401-3818
USA

www.ashgate.com

British Library Cataloguing in Publication Data
Bennett, Zoë.
  Using the Bible in practical theology : historical and
  contemporary perspectives. – (Explorations in practical,
  pastoral and empirical theology)
  1. Theology, Practical. 2. Bible – Use. 3. Bible and
  sociology. 4. Ruskin, John, 1819–1900.
  I. Title II. Series
  253–dc23

The Library of Congress has cataloged the printed edition as follows:
Bennett, Zoë.
  Using the Bible in practical theology : historical and contemporary perspectives / by Zoë
Bennett.
    pages cm. – (Explorations in practical, pastoral, and empirical theology)
  Includes bibliographical references and index.
  1. Bible – Hermeneutics. 2. Bible – Use. 3. Theology, Practical. I. Title.
  BS476.B446 2013
  250–dc23

2012049674

ISBN   9781409437925 (hbk)
ISBN   9781409437932 (ebk-PDF)
ISBN   9781472401496 (ebk-ePUB)

Reprinted 2014

Printed in the United Kingdom by Henry Ling Limited, at the Dorset Press, Dorchester, DT1 1HD

For Isabelle, Naomi and Abigail

*ὁ δὲ ἀνεξέταστος βίος οὐ βιωτὸς ἀνθρώπῳ – for a human being the
unexamined life is not worth living.*
(Socrates, Apologia 38a)

*"Nein", sagte der Zwerg, "lasst uns vom Menschen reden! Etwas
Lebendiges ist mir lieber als alle Schätze der Welt!" – "No", said the
dwarf, "let us talk about human beings! Something living is dearer to me
than all the treasure in the world!"*
(Brothers Grimm, 'Rumpelstiltskin')

Without contraries there is no progression.
(William Blake, The Marriage of Heaven and Hell)

Contents

Acknowledgements

Heartfelt thanks are due to the following people:

To colleagues with whom I shared this year the joys of teaching biblical hermeneutics, and for conversations in the car between Cambridge and Chelmsford: Susan Durber, Philip Jenson and especially Ela Lazarewicz-Wyrzykowska.

To my companions in the great adventure of the Professional Doctorate: Elaine Graham, David Lyall, Stephen Pattison, Vernon Trafford and Heather Walton.

To my closest colleagues every day: Amy Barnett, Alison Burling, Esther Shreeve and Rowena Small – for friendship, support and encouragement, and for listening to me endlessly chattering about this book.

To Mark Cartledge, who many years ago challenged me to think of trust as an important category and practice in biblical hermeneutics.

To colleagues and students in the Cambridge Theological Federation and to Andrew Rogers and colleagues in BIAPT and the Bible and Practical Theology Special Interest Group, for the grace of communities in which difference may be held and practised with dignity and joy.

To three friends who have read and commented on the text in part or in whole, and thus have shared the final part of the journey with me – for this labour and for many conversations about the Bible in the past: Paul Ballard, Margaret Elliot and Chris Rowland.

To Martyn Percy, and to Sarah Lloyd, Tricia Craggs and others at Ashgate, for gracious help in the production and publishing of this book, and to Abigail Humphries for indexing.

To my daughters Isabelle, Naomi and Abigail, to whom this book is dedicated, for love and companionship.

Introduction

The Origins of this Book

This book has its origins in my own struggle with the Bible. I grew up an Anglican 'open evangelical', 'learning' my Christian faith in the 1960s in the church youth group, and in my university days did valiant, though rather immature, battle with, on the one hand, those more conservative than myself who espoused the 'verbal inerrancy' of the Bible and, on the other, those who seemed to me to blunt the true evangelical witness in uncritical ecumenical mixing. Fifteen years later, when I returned to postgraduate study in Cambridge, my question was still 'what kind of animal is the Bible?' By now it was a question; and a question of serious personal and existential importance for me. Could I trust the Bible? Could I feel confident that through the Bible I might know truth about God, about the world and about how to live? And what should I do about competing interpretations? It felt to me as if my capacity to know *anything* for sure was implicated in this question of the Bible, which was the foundation of my faith; and the threat of meaninglessness was emotionally as well as intellectually frightening.

Behind this it seemed to me there lay a series of questions concerning truth, and our capacity as human beings to know anything as true: What can we know? Can we talk meaningfully of 'revelation'? Can we know anything truly about God, and if so how? The reader may note that my education at this point included grappling with the critique of human knowing posed by Immanuel Kant (1724–1804), and the key question of how anything could be said to be true beyond what was discerned by our five senses on the one hand and the way our human brain orders what comes to it on the other.

I have never lost either of the dispositions towards the Bible that are sketched here, and they deeply inform the passion behind this book. First, there is a rootedness in the Bible and a sense of its richness and its capacity to reveal to us truth about ourselves, about other people, the world and God. Second, there is a willingness to ask radical questions, even those that shake us out of our securities, and to live with doubt and complexity.

I came across John Ruskin by accident. The university I work for took his name – Anglia Ruskin University. Ruskin had given the inaugural lecture when the earliest part of our university, the Cambridge School of Art, was founded in

October 1858.[1] Intrigued by the way every department seemed to claim an interest in this polymath – art, English literature, politics, history – I set out to see what interest Ruskin held for practical theology. I found treasure. I found a man who read the Bible in medieval Greek manuscripts daily, and annotated them in ink. I found a man for whom sight was the most precious of our senses:

> [T]he greatest thing a human soul ever does in this world is to *see* something, and tell what it saw in a plain way. Hundreds of people can talk for one who can think, but thousands can think for one who can see. To see clearly is poetry, prophecy, and religion, – all in one.[2]

Gold dust for the practical theologian.

Not only this, but I found a man with an extraordinary capacity to live with doubt, yet whose engagement with the Bible was robust, imaginative, centrally important to him and richly fruitful in the public domain. After my first visit to the British Library to look at Ruskin's annotations on the medieval Greek Lectionary he owned I recorded, 'The way Ruskin treated the text in this manuscript shows a man so utterly at home in the text of the Bible that he could afford to question, even be contemptuous, without losing his relationship with it.' Something he wrote in an open letter illustrates the point perfectly:

> My good wiseacre readers, I know as many flaws in the book of Genesis as the best of you, but I knew the book before I knew its flaws, while you know the flaws, and never have known the book, nor can know it.[3]

Here was a man who lived constantly with questions about the Bible, agonising public and personal questions, but for whom it was a companion and a source of prophetic public passion all his life. Chapter 4 will tell more of the story of Ruskin, and chapters 5–8 more of why he can so brilliantly illuminate our use of the Bible in practical and public theology.

The Heart of this Book

I suppose that this heading should really read 'the heart and stomach of this book', because there are two places from which it takes life, energy and the power to work.

---

[1]   Produced by Anglia Ruskin University, October 2006 as *Mr. Ruskin's Inaugural Address Delivered at Cambridge Oct.29th, 1858*; see also *Works*, 16, 177–201. Quotations from Ruskin's published works are taken from the Library Edition: E.T. Cook and A. Wedderburn (eds), *The Works of John Ruskin*, 39 vols (London: George Allen, 1903–12), referred to as *Works*, volume and page number.

[2]   *Works*, 5, 333.

[3]   *Works*, 28, 85.

The first is my lifelong engagement with Christian nurture and with various formal and informal types of 'theological education'. The second is my conviction that John Ruskin (1819–1900) has something to offer practical and public theology, and that this choice of a nineteenth-century figure to explore is not arbitrary, but leads us into ways of engagement between contemporary life and the Bible that are rigorous, illuminating and creative.

For 17 years I have directed an MA course in pastoral theology, and for six years a Professional Doctorate in practical theology, and this, together with my membership, as a Reader, of the Church of England, has convinced me that one of the deepest needs in the area of public practical theology is a thoughtful, imaginative, persuasive and hermeneutically sophisticated use of the Bible. I have written this book primarily for people in the churches, clergy and lay, who are wrestling with how the Bible can be appropriately related to the everyday events and problems with which they are engaged, and it is also designed for the increasing number of students in formal theological education, and particularly Masters and DMin/Professional Doctorate courses, who need to engage with the Bible in a hermeneutically sophisticated manner in relation to the contemporary issues with which they are dealing.

I have found that practising Christians of all shades of ecclesial tradition will naturally and quickly turn to the Bible in their studies of practical theology; but in that turn a range of problems surface. Such problems manifest themselves as both personal and intellectual-critical, and these two aspects are often deeply entangled. The class whose every meeting ended in wrestling with how, if at all, we understood 'biblical authority'; the woman who could not bear to use the Bible in an assessment liturgy as this course was the only place she had found where she could name the way the Bible had been used to damage her, and the other woman for whom the Bible had been all her life the place of refuge from abuse; the man who came into the class bringing 30 years of ministry experience, who loved the Bible but no longer knew how to connect it meaningfully with his pastoral work – all these and many more have contributed to this book.

Helen Cameron and her colleagues, in their recent book *Theological Reflection for Human Flourishing*, offer us a fascinating demonstration of exactly the problem I have identified. While the participants in their action learning event, who were pastors and people working on the church–public sector interface, had no problems engaging in a lively and fluent way with psychological and sociological perspectives, they became uneasy and silent, and the process became constipated, as soon as they attempted to engage with the Bible. There were liberal scruples, practical problems, internal hesitations, fears of external non-acceptance and recourse to an external 'expert' to 'solve' the problem. When an experienced group of Christian ministers can handle secular disciplines with confidence but have this deep reticence about the Bible we have a brilliant indication of a real problem in our midst: 'given the chronic nature of the problem that practitioners have struggling to make connections with the Bible, ve attempted to set up a process which sought to take seriously this problem and bring the issue to the surface'.[4]

Alongside formal theological education I have had a lifetime's experience of engaging with the Bible in the church and beyond it, in situations of Christian nurture and education. Three contexts of practice have particularly shaped my understanding. The first is my early involvement with young people's work, specifically with Christian 'houseparties' – residential events for 14–18 year olds – run by our own parish church and more widely under the auspices of CYFA (Church Youth Fellowships Association). Here I learned the excitement and power of a love for the Bible and a use of the Bible that sustained and challenged everyday lives. Later on in life concerns emerged for me about a reading of the Bible that had little sense of either the possibilities of human ideological distortion or the multiplicity of interpretation; but the raw and living engagement with the text, day after day, built a foundation of biblical knowledge and, more significantly, the capacity to connect this text, our own life and the living God.

As a 'young mum' and 'vicar's wife' in the 1970s and 1980s I was involved in several flourishing 'young mums' church groups. One particular venture stands out in which we had, in addition to our more general social gathering, a Bible Study group once a fortnight – or rather several Bible Study groups. There were four, and one was reserved, by their own request, for enquirers rather than committed Christians. Nothing unusual in that, but what has never left me is the shock of myself moving from group to group and noticing how the level of honesty, curiosity, critical questioning, even excitement, was so much higher in the enquirers' group. It was as if Christian commitment somehow dulled the sharpness of what could be thought and named, required a certain 'diplomacy' before God and before fellow Christians in what could be said, and contracted the range of the imagination. The sense that this does happen, and that it is a terrible shame, has never left me, and has been my experience in the years since then.

As a Reader in the Church of England, I regularly preach. Preaching is a place where we have to put public words to where we are in relation to the Bible, we have to own what we say. It has for me been a place where my struggles with faith and with the Bible, whether generated by my personal life or by the horrific conditions pertaining in the world, have had to be dealt with responsibly, with honesty towards the text of the Bible, towards the realities of the world and towards my own understanding and feelings.

The second heart, or driving conviction, behind this book has been a delighted obsession with the work of John Ruskin. Ruskin was a public figure of enormous impact, and his work is being taken up today in many fields – for example economic, educational and ecological. His engagement was political and economic, aesthetic and ethical, and was in all respects throughout his life deeply biblically informed.

---

4   Helen Cameron, John Reader and Victoria Slater with Christopher Rowland, *Theological Reflection for Human Flourishing* (London: SCM Press, 2012), p. 87, see the whole of chapter 5.

Using Ruskin's work in a systematic way enables us by analogy to reflect on the processes of our own interpretation and use of the Bible.

So the approach I take in the book is deliberately oblique and analogical, in that it looks at biblical hermeneutics through analysis and reflection on this outstanding writer on public life. The central Part II considers the way in which John Ruskin used the Bible. This enables readers to see for themselves how the different aspects of this distinguished critic's work, immersed as he was in the Bible, combine to offer a rich interpretative method.

The reason for using Ruskin in this way is that it illuminates the central point of Hans-Georg Gadamer's hermeneutics: the contingency of all biblical reading.[5] The critical distance afforded by the historical example enables us to recognise better the contingent nature of our own hermeneutical preferences and training, and the ways in which our context determines interpretation. So, readers will be introduced to the biblical theology of a major figure in nineteenth-century cultural and political life, and invited to see how engagement with the Bible in theology always requires respect for both poles of the interpretative task – modern context and ancient text – and will be offered appropriate analytical tools to engage in a critically aware understanding. The book, therefore, seeks to exemplify in its own approach the nature of practical theology. All of us can go to the Bible, but too often we do so without being aware of the lenses through which we are reading, whether academic or existential. The use of the Bible in the influential writing of Ruskin can not only enable us to see how he went about it but also how he too was a man of his time, with a range of assumptions about what the Bible meant and cultural and social presuppositions different from our own. Thereby we may comprehend and reflect on the nature of our prejudices, which influence our reading.

The Contribution of this Book to Practical and Public Theology

Part I starts with a series of cameos that foreground the centrality of the text/ experience connection as it has existed from the very beginnings of the Christian faith and also indicate the problems and the disruptions of our encounters with the Bible, as text and life are related. The starting point is deliberately personal, existential and self-involving. Tensions and differences are explored, and two families of traditions identified, one seeking to evade the 'tyranny of experience' and the other the 'tyranny of the text'. Part II looks at how John Ruskin provides an example for negotiation of our relationship with the Bible, both of 'playing' with text and of working with it with deep seriousness in the public square. Part III takes what has been learned, working with it and adding to it in relation to contemporary texts, which themselves engage deeply with the Bible. The Kairos Palestine document addresses one of the most crucial public issues of our time and is rooted in a biblical

---

[5]   See Chapter 2.

lerstanding, while also appealing to constituencies wider than the Christian community. In particular, it deals with an issue where the interpretation of the Bible is contentious, because the received text includes not only the liberation of an enslaved people but their elimination of the indigenous population, and thus makes the handling of the biblical text problematic and requiring a nuanced hermeneutical approach. The *Guardian* interview with Giles Fraser at the time of his resignation from St Paul's Cathedral over the expulsion of the Occupy London camp represents a quite different kind of text – more ephemeral and 'on the hoof' – and thus illustrates a quite different kind of public theology and use of the Bible. The final chapter seeks to draw together the differing strands of the book in a return to the personal and autobiographical with which it started, and in an example and an analysis of how the process of critical self-reflection is at the heart of biblical hermeneutics and of practical theology.

This book is situated, broadly speaking, within the discipline of practical theology, so the starting point is indeed the person with the Bible in one hand and the newspaper in the other. The heart of the subject matter is expressed in four elements: the importance of informed seeing, the capacity to be a reader of multiple texts, the internalising of the biblical text, and making the fruits of theological reflection do work in the public realm. It locates the use of the Bible within the conversation that goes on between tradition and experience, and also within the conversation between secular and theological disciplines, which typifies all forms of modern practical theology. As the argument of the book unfolds further 'texts' appear. Beginning with two texts – the text of the Bible and the text of life – the book adds two more, the 'reflective text' and the 'performed text'. The practical theologian's role is both as reflector and as actor. This is a true 'action-reflection' model, which gives shape to the whole book and is demonstrated in microcosm in the final chapter, which is a reflective text about my own 'performance', in community, of the relationship between the text of the Bible and the text of life.

This practical theology is also public. The expression 'public theology' has a specific resonance in the present context, and I do not wish either to claim special expertise in or to confine what I write to that resonance. But I do wish wholeheartedly to claim the public nature of most practical theology that is done, and the practical nature of most public theology.

> This is an extraordinary moment for those of us who have been engaged in theological reflection on public issues around the world in recent decades. With the launch of the *International Journal of Public Theology* and the *Global Network for Public Theology* in 2007, we may speak of this year as a 'kairos moment' for this emerging research field.[6]

---

[6]   W. Storrar, '2007: A Kairos Moment for Public Theology', *International Journal of Public Theology*, 1.1 (2007): 5–25, at 5. For the Global Network for Public Theology, see http://www.csu.edu.au/special/accc/about/gnpt/home. The British and Irish Association of Practical Theology has recently formed a Special Interest Group in Public Theology.

So began Will Storrar in the first article in the first *International Journal of Public Theology*, marking the coming of age and public self-awareness of a specific activity within theology and among theologians. He identifies three factors as being constitutive of this public theology: that it is *collaborative* theological reflection on public issues; that it begins in *disruptive issues* such as conflict and suffering; and that it draws on the *methodology of practical theology*, with its roots in the pastoral cycle of reflection on experience and its heart in human concerns that call for a pastoral response. Public theology includes all reflection in a public context on matters of public concern: medicine and money, the local skateboarding facility and the Olympics, the church and the village. While public theology includes that theology that emanates from church leaders, think-tanks, reports and professional theologians, it is also the activity of countless men and women week-in week-out, in pulpits, in local activism or in regular practices of engagement with the world.

In May 2012 the British and Irish Association of Practical Theology (BIAPT) held the first symposium for a newly formed Special Interest Group on 'the Bible and practical theology'. For the first time in the history of BIAPT it brought together researching professionals and reflective practitioners from all over the constituency, and crucially from a range of ecclesial backgrounds and 'churchpersonship'.[7] It felt to us that things were moving, that 'the Bible' was no longer the elephant in the room of practical theology.[8] Those who spoke of 'the tyranny of experience' and those who spoke of 'the tyranny of the text' were speaking to each other. We were sharing personal and professional stories and, to our surprise and delight, we hugely enjoyed actually reading the Bible together. To this ongoing movement of rapprochement, wherever it is found, I dedicate this book.

---

[7]   This was for some of us a continuation of the work begun in the Use of the Bible and Pastoral Practice project organised jointly by the Bible Society and the University of Cardiff. The influence and work of Paul Ballard in this process has been crucial, and his article in the Wiley-Blackwell Companion is an excellent summary of the current state of the use of the Bible in practical theology: 'The Use of Scripture', in Bonnie J. Miller-McLemore (ed.), *The Wiley-Blackwell Companion to Practical Theology* (Oxford: Wiley-Blackwell, 2011), pp. 163–72.

[8]   Stephen Pattison, *A Critique of Pastoral Care*, 3rd edn (London: SCM Press, 2000), chapter 6.

PART I
Using the Bible – the Reader of Multiple Texts

The Bible itself offers a paradigmatic story of struggle to us: Jacob wrestling with God all night at the ford of the Jabbok.

> *Jacob was left alone; and a man wrestled with him until daybreak. When the man saw that he did not prevail against Jacob, he struck him on the hip socket; and Jacob's hip was put out of joint as he wrestled with him. Then he said, 'Let me go, for the day is breaking.' But Jacob said, 'I will not let you go, unless you bless me.' (Gen. 32.24–6)*

Two chapters earlier in this story we hear of one of Jacob's wives, Rachel, also wrestling:

> *Rachel's maid Bilhah conceived again and bore Jacob a second son. Then Rachel said, 'With mighty wrestlings I have wrestled with my sister, and have prevailed'; so she named him Naphtali. (Gen. 30.7–8)*

The word 'wrestle' translates two different Hebrew words, one evoking ground or dust, the other evoking entwined-ness and tortuousness. Jacob wrestles with God and alone, the night before he meets his brother; the story of Rachel's wrestlings with her sister is more communal and down to earth, in the daily pain of infertility and of a polygamous marriage, and of childbirth in which she eventually dies. Two human stories, a man's story and a woman's story, which together bring out the struggle of human life as we come to understand it and begin to be able to live with ourselves, with our sisters and brothers and with God. Wrestling with the Bible, I will argue, is for Christians a normal experience in communal and individual discipleship – even if it is not always recognised as such. Jacob wrestling with God is a poignant symbol of this struggle for many of us, men and women, though perhaps Rachel's wrestling with her sister and co-wife, and her infertility, is an image more pertinent to others, less heroic and more embedded in daily life.

In this book I have deliberately chosen to enter the hermeneutical circle of text and life, at the point of struggle. I have begun with the contemporary human interpreters, in places of struggle – struggle to make sense of the Bible in the midst of our lives and in relationship to others – places where people reach an impasse, individually or communally, and where they question.

In Chapter 2 I follow this up by examining our situation as readers of these texts, recognising our struggle and exploring the nature of our self-involvement.

Chapter 3 introduces the tension, indeed sometimes the struggle, in our different approaches to the text of the Bible and the 'text' of life, examining the places of critique and of commitment, of suspicion and of trust.

By beginning this book with the struggles readers have with the text of the Bible I place myself on a well-used map, which delineates three key areas in the territory 'biblical interpretation': the author, the text and the reader, or the world behind the text, the world in the text and the world in front of the text.[1]

The author area of the map includes questions such as date and authorship of the text, historical information and the contemporary world view at the time of writing, or of the oral tradition represented in that writing. This area of the map is the traditional terrain of the biblical historical critic. It has been the staple diet of biblical scholars and their students in the western world since the nineteenth century and has its roots in the rise of scientific and historical understanding in the Enlightenment. The reader area of the map covers the contemporary world of the reader rather than the ancient historical world of the writer, focusing on how the text is read and interpreted, by whom, and what the world looks like from their point of view. It includes interest in how a reader responds to the text, and in how a reader applies the text in their own situation. Taken together these two areas of the map are often known as the 'two horizons' of interpretation. It is in the relationship between these, the fusion of them or in the creative tension between them that meaning-making and practical application takes place. The third area of the map is the text itself. For example, in literary criticism of the Bible or in Canonical Criticism, the text itself as it stands is the focus of attention.

---

[1]   See further Craig Bartholomew, Colin Greene and Karl Möller, *Renewing Biblical Interpretation* (Carlisle: Paternoster, 2000); John Barton, 'Classifying Biblical Criticism', *Journal for the Study of the Old Testament*, 29 (1984): 19–35; David A. Holgate and Rachel Starr, *SCM Study Guide to Biblical Hermeneutics* (London: SCM Press, 2006); Manfred Oeming, *Contemporary Biblical Hermeneutics: An Introduction*, trans. Joachim F. Vette (Aldershot: Ashgate, 2006); Andrew Village, *The Bible and Lay People: An Empirical Approach to Ordinary Hermeneutics* (Aldershot: Ashgate, 2007).

Chapter 1

The Text of the Bible and the Text of Life

What Happens When We Read the Bible?

I want to start with real people. Each of the cameos in this section is from the lives of ordinary people. I have chosen them to illustrate how Christians struggle to find their way as they seek with real and often painful seriousness to understand how the Bible shapes their life, and the lives of others, and conversely how their life shapes their understanding of the Bible. The first is my own story.

Cameo One – What Can I Believe?

In 1988 I was sitting in the vicarage front room, my own front room, excited and a little shy and unnerved. This was one of my first days of 'freedom', as my youngest child had just started school. Fourteen years previously I had graduated from Cambridge with a degree in Classics and Theology. Since then I had been a vicar's wife and a mother – happy in these roles, and using my theological understanding and my teaching gifts in the service of the church in a voluntary capacity. I had begun to be disturbed by that debate between the inerrancy and the infallibility of the Bible. Brought up an open evangelical, how did I cope with the challenge that if you did not believe the Bible was verbally absolutely accurate and trustworthy in all matters, geographical and historical as well as ethical, how could you be sure of anything? Until this point I had operated with a de facto infallibility position, a pragmatic approach to living informed by daily devotional reading of the Bible and trying to live by its commands and promises as interpreted to me by the evangelical culture I inhabited. But now I began to think more deeply. I was very much attracted by the inerrancy argument, that a belief in a sovereign God who was utterly trustworthy implied belief that He was competent and willing to reveal Himself without error, and to enable us to receive that revelation.[1] By contrast, the 'infallibility' position, that the Bible was infallible in matters of ethics and belief but not necessarily inerrant in matters of history, geography and science, felt as if it left me open to a domino effect – once I stopped believing one

---

[1] As classically expressed in a piece of writing that meant much to me at the time, Cornelius Van Til's introduction to B.B.Warfield, *The Inspiration and Authority of the Bible*, ed. Samuel G. Craig (Philadelphia: Presbyterian and Reformed Publishing, 1948).

thing all the rest would tumble. Existentially I found this very frightening indeed. Though now, as I write this in my late fifties, I find it difficult to access the level of fear I felt then, I know that my 35-year-old self was terrified, and felt on the edge of mental breakdown, by the threat to my sense that I could be sure of anything. It was a religious crisis, an epistemological vortex in which everything I trusted felt threatened. While the trigger varies, the experience is common: the beliefs that sustained our young selves are inadequate for the adult self. This is not just about our intellect but also about our emotions, and even our sense of identity. 'God' who seemed so like a rock now felt like a floating island in a storm. The 'seasickness' was appalling.

I had begun to study theology again, back in Cambridge, to which I had recently moved. This compounded the sense of terror in one way, but in another way it gave me a language in which to order my thoughts and feelings. And so I return to that early afternoon seminar in the sunny vicarage lounge, surrounded by my colleagues and friends, about a dozen of us, discussing our work as evangelical-identified postgraduate students with a great guru of the evangelical movement. My moment had come to ask an evangelical guru my burning existential question: 'since all knowledge is received by us as human beings, processed by us, understood and shaped by our human minds, what does it mean to talk about revelation from God? Doesn't it all come from us? Don't we construct knowledge? Or at the very least, isn't it all apprehended by our faculties and given meaning by how we understand it?'

His answer has never left me: 'I thought we were all evangelicals here.'

Reflection
This cameo highlights several key issues about reading the Bible. First, we change and grow. We are nurtured in a certain way of understanding our faith, including what the Bible means to us, and as we change, grow older and experience more of life, our understanding grows too, otherwise we burst out of it like the wine out of old wineskins or as we do out of our old clothes. That is emphatically *not* to say that our faith or our understanding of the Bible will become less deep, less strong or less important to us; it is just to say it will change. If it does not, we will experience either cognitive and emotional dissonance, in which part of us feels uncomfortably out of step with another part of us, or 'splitting', in which we suppress, ignore and hide away a part of us we cannot face up to. How we manage this growth is fundamentally important.

Second, we manage this growth and wrestle with these questions in relationship to the communities of faith that have nurtured us, that have taught us how to read the Bible and to which we belong. It is of those we trust, and in the company of those we trust, that we can ask questions. Sometimes that is extremely difficult and painful and may result in exclusion. My exclusion has been after many years partially redeemed, but not all such stories have a happy ending. It is also with the tools, intellectual, spiritual and emotional, that we have acquired through what we have learned thus far that we can make the next moves and take the next steps.

Third, questions about the Bible matter to us; they are existentially important, not just 'academic'. In this case my question mattered to me as an all-embracing question about how I could trust the word of God to me, indeed, how I could be sure of anything. Sometimes our questions are ethical and practical, about sexual ethics or political violence for example; sometimes they are deeply emotionally important, what do we believe has happened to a loved one who has died?

Fourth, this incident crystallized for me the centrality of the question of revelation. Twenty years of teaching theology and working in the church have not changed my view that whether anything is revealed by God, if so how and if so what, are fundamental issues for theology and for Christian belief and practice.

Finally, the BIAPT Special Interest Group which I mentioned in the Introduction was for me a kind of recapitulation of this incident – a coming home. I told the story in these words as my contribution to the symposium. It was not a coming home in the sense of a return to where I was then, but a spiralling, as is appropriate for a practical theologian, to a new place, in which the polarisations of that time had given way to a more fluid engagement, more able to accept contraries – contraries within myself and contraries within a group, and indeed within the Bible itself. It was a place where this story was accepted, along with other people's stories, and critically reflected on, with the purpose of moving forwards collaboratively.

Cameo Two – Violence and the Bible

My class was discussing whether the injunction in Colossians and 1 Peter that wives should be obedient to their husbands was a contributory cause of domestic violence in some Christian households. Most of the people in the room found it incredible. Then a woman spoke up quietly and said, 'For seventeen years my husband used these verses to justify beating me.' In the silence that ensued, a beam spread across her face: 'But the Holy Spirit told me he was wrong!'

Reflection
There are two crucial issues raised by this cameo. In the first place, there are portions of the Bible that have been used to justify actions that many Christians, on grounds they would see as in themselves essentially Christian, abhor. This raises two further questions. One, would it be true to say that some parts of the Bible, for example those that seem to justify violence, are in tension with other parts? Is the Bible itself a site of struggle?[2] Two, is it right to think that here the Bible itself carries the blame or is it that people, such as this woman's husband,

---

[2]   See Itumeleng J. Mosala, *Biblical Hermeneutics and Black Theology in South Africa* (Grand Rapids, Mich.: W.B. Eerdmans, 1989).

have wrongly interpreted it and the Bible itself is exonerated?[3] How many people have to make that wrong interpretation for the original text to carry some blame?[4]

Then there is the question of the Holy Spirit. This woman was giving living testimony to that interaction between the written text and the living presence, indeed voice, of God in human life, which is of the essence of Christianity, Calvin's 'testimonium internum'.[5] She was also offering her witness, and that witness was being corroborated by the community that heard her, that her husband's interpretation had violated not only herself but the spirit of the Christian gospel of love. This is to assume there is a 'canon within the canon'; that it is possible to identify, within the scriptures and the Christian tradition, a 'heart of the gospel', to which other interpretations are subject.

This cameo gives a specific and startling instance of our claim that we read the Bible through and in the Spirit of God, that the Bible was written through the inspiration of the Spirit of God, and that the individual is part of the interpretative community inspired by the same Spirit of God. It also causes us to recognise that alternative and contradictory interpretations will arise and be enacted.

Cameo Three – The Preacher and the Bible

He sat opposite me and said with passion, 'That will be no use at all to me when I preach to my congregation in Uganda. It will be worse than useless.' I was arguing with him over whether we found violence in the biblical text, and what we did with 'texts of terror' like the command to wipe out the Canaanites or the story of Jephthah's daughter.[6] My own experience, that understanding how the Bible itself has violence embedded in the text is liberative, was not his. He explained: 'I am a preacher and a pastor. In my congregation there is too much violence – domestic and other violence. The Bible is the rule of faith, revered and authoritative. It is vital to me, utterly committed as I am to preventing violence, to be able to preach unequivocally that the gospel, and the teachings of the Bible, condemn violence.'

Reflection
I was tempted to answer that he would never win, that because the Bible does not unequivocally condemn violence, how did he know the Bible text itself would not

---

3   See Carole R. Fontaine, 'The Abusive Bible: On the Use of Feminist Methods in Pastoral Contexts', in Athalya Brenner and Carole Fontaine (eds), *A Feminist Companion to Reading the Bible: Approaches, Methods and Strategies* (Sheffield: Sheffield Academic Press, 1997), pp. 84–113.

4   See WCC, *Living Letters: A Report of Visits to the Churches during the Ecumenical Decade – Churches in Solidarity with Women* (Geneva: WCC, 1997).

5   John Calvin, *Institutes of the Christian Religion*, ed. John T. McNeill, Library of Christian Classics 20, 21 (London: SCM Press, 1961), I.vii.4–5; see 1 Cor. 2.

6   Phyllis Trible, *Texts of Terror: Literary-feminist Readings of Biblical Narratives* (Philadelphia: Fortress Press, 1984).

win out over his selective preaching of it? But then how was I so sure that the deep message of the crucified one, not to mention of this Christian preacher's life, would not win out over the 'texts of terror'? What is embedded in this conversation is not only the issue of cross-cultural (mis)understanding, but, more fundamentally, the issue of the complex dialectical relationship between the text itself, the preaching of the text, and human lives and experiences.

He was describing to me a context, not an unusual one, in which the primary medium through which people receive the Bible is preaching. It is mediated through a figure who has authority in the church, and it is mediated in an authoritative way. He was also describing honestly a situation in which, while the prima facie belief would be that the Bible was being taken literally and at face value, the reality would be that he, the authoritative preacher, was deliberately ignoring certain facets of the Bible, in order to promote a particular understanding and specific ways of behaving which he believed to be of the essence of the gospel message. This is something most preachers do all the time, though with less self-awareness than my Ugandan colleague.

Cameo Four – Going 'the Extra Mile'

Six older people talk together of how the Bible and the world are related. It is a Lent group. They have been asked to talk about the struggles of their daily lives, and they come alive as they share stories – looking after aged and sick parents, being put upon at work, 'going the extra mile'. They are not the world's rich and successful; they are the salt of the earth. 'That's it', they say, 'we are always being asked "to go the extra mile".' When the discussion leader tells them that 'going the extra mile' is a quotation from the Bible, that it is what Jesus told us to do, their surprise and delight is evident – 'Really?!', they say.

Reflection

These are church people; they go to Parish Eucharist every week. They hear the Bible read there. Their faith is not intellectual; it is practical. They go the extra mile for their neighbours, their families, their friends and their employers. What issues does this cameo raise?

First, the Bible captures the imagination. They don't even remember the phrase is from the Bible, but it fires them. It gives them a way of understanding their lives. It gives them a sense that what they do is part of a bigger picture of goodness.

Second, the Bible is about action. It is about what we do in our daily lives. It is about tending the sick, giving to others even when you are exhausted, living out what you believe to be right.

But third, this also has a more ambiguous side; it is for them about being the little people, the people taken advantage of by their employers. This ambiguity is also buried in the diverse possible interpretations of what is going on in the biblical passage from which the expression comes.

Finally, so much is implicit. Here is this phrase which is originally about being forced to walk a mile with the occupying forces. None of them knew that. That didn't matter. The phrase has come into English usage, meaning to do above and beyond the call of duty, for love. They found in the Bible, without even knowing it, a way of expressing what they did, with pain and struggle, both knowing it to be part of loving service to humanity and also feeling the injustice and the ambiguity.

Cameo Five – Introducing John Ruskin: The Private and the Public

> I notice in one of your late letters some notion that I am coming to think the Bible 'the word of God' – because I use it – out of Rosie's book – for daily teaching … – But I never was farther from thinking – and never can be nearer to, thinking, any thing of the sort. Nothing could ever persuade me that God writes vulgar Greek … If there is any divine truth at all in the mixed collection of books which we call a Bible, that truth is, that the Word of God comes *directly* to different people in different ways … [t]hat cross in the sky … in the clouds … and the calm sky … by and through the words of *any* book … the Word of God may come to us: and because I love Rosie so, I *think* God does teach me, every morning, by her lips, through her book.[7]

Reflection

We have here moved back 150 years, from contemporary examples to 1867, when John Ruskin wrote this, to his younger cousin and dear friend Joan Severn.[8] Rosie (Rose La Touche) was a young woman, many years Ruskin's junior, with whom he had a troubled and ultimately tragic romantic relationship which gave him deep pain. She was a devout Christian of evangelical persuasion and longed to draw him into conservatively orthodox Christian faith, to which end she bombarded him with biblical texts. What he says in this letter to his cousin needs to be read against a background of personal involvement and conflicting emotions.

We do not come to the Bible in a vacuum; it already has a context in our lives, including a personal context. We have a history of our engagement with it which may involve love and hate, struggle and joy. We have a network of relationships with other people, whose attitudes to the Bible, positive or negative, affect us – not least our parents, and behind them our upbringing. Ruskin was a man who knew not only the enrichment but also the pain of self-involvement in the text of the Bible.

---

[7]   Rachel Dickinson (ed.), *John Ruskin's Correspondence with Joan Severn: Sense and Nonsense Letters* (London: Modern Humanities Research Association and Maney Publishing, 2009), pp. 88–9. Ruskin's love for 'Rosie' and its relationship to his reading of the Bible is further expanded in Zoë Bennett, '"By Fors, thus blotted with a double cross": Some Notes upon the Death of Rose La Touche', *Ruskin Review and Bulletin*, 5.2 (Autumn 2009): 27–34.

[8]   I have mentioned John Ruskin in the Introduction, and will say much more about him in Part II.

Agony over the Bible included more than his relationship with Rose. His faith was shaped by a strict evangelical upbringing, as an only son learning and reciting the Bible everyday at his mother's knee, and by his ultimate rebellion against that – a shaping and a rebellion that cut to the heart of his deepest personality and most intimate relationships. Furthermore, the context of these inner personal and relational struggles was the Victorian world in which the 'geologist's hammer', the discoveries and evolutionary theory of Darwin, and the philosophical and historical criticism of the Bible all conspired to shake the faith of the believer. This passage demonstrates how he puts the revelation of God through the Bible into a context of a wider and more general revelation through nature or through any other book.

In 1867 Ruskin gave a succinct public account of Victorian attitudes to the Bible, describing them as 'four possible Theories respecting the Authority of the Bible':

- those for whom every word of the book known to them as the Bible was dictated by a Supreme Being
- those for whom the substance of the Bible was given by divine inspiration, containing infallibly all that is necessary for salvation ('held by our good and upright clergymen, and the better class of the professedly religious laity')
- those who believed that the Bible was like other human writings in origin, mixing truth and error, but bearing true witness to the dealings of God with the human race, to the life, miracles and resurrection of Christ and to the 'life of the world to come'
- those who held that the scriptures were no more authoritative than other religious understandings, expressive of the 'enthusiastic visions of beliefs of earnest men oppressed by the world's darkness', but that they were 'to be reverently studied, as containing a portion, divinely appointed, of the best wisdom which human intellect earnestly seeking for help from God, has hitherto been able to gather between birth and death'.[9]

Ruskin implicitly counts himself among these last at this stage of his life. Here is a brilliant externalised account of contemporary Victorian attitudes to the Bible.

I have set out these two positions of Ruskin's – the objective external analysis of his own and his contemporaries' attitudes to the Bible, and his analysis of his personal subjective investment and practice – as an invitation to see how self-involvement sits alongside objective reading – God speaks to him here, as he said, 'because I love Rosie so'. It also shows how reflection on our reading may enrich our understanding of it. Ruskin is poignantly self-aware of how his reading of the Bible is entangled with his love for Rose; and in being so self-aware, and in laying it out so succinctly and honestly, he enables himself and us to see something of the complex and potentially revelatory relationship between the reader, the text and, indeed, the Spirit of God. Ruskin was a man who related to his Bible in a deeply

---

[9]   *Works*, 17, 348–50.

personal way in the midst of doubts and crises of faith. His attitude to the Bible was warm and playful, he could take it to task as a friend, he could be alternately moved and angry, challenged and scornful.

In the Beginning: Experience and the Bible

Starting first with my own experience and then that of others, contemporary and historical, was quite deliberate. I want to anchor this book in two things: first the necessity for a reflective and critical look at ourselves in our already existing relationships to the Bible and to the people and the communities who have mediated it to us; second the conviction that the centrality of experience to interpretation of the Bible is not an alien, imported feature but is fundamental to the very origins of scripture. The first Christians started with their experience. Part of that experience, as part of mine and of the other people in my cameos, was precisely our scriptures – for us our Bible, for the early Jewish Christians the Jewish scriptures which they went on to call the Old Testament.

Cameo Six – Interpretation from the Start: Relating the 'Old' and the 'New'

Paul the Apostle, once Saul the Pharisee, writes from Ephesus to the Christians in Corinth, around 55 CE:

> I do not want you to be unaware, brothers and sisters, that our ancestors were all under the cloud, and all passed through the sea, and all were baptized into Moses in the cloud and in the sea, and all ate the same spiritual food, and all drank the same spiritual drink. For they drank from the spiritual rock that followed them, and the rock was Christ. Nevertheless, God was not pleased with most of them, and they were struck down in the wilderness.
>
> Now these things occurred as examples for us, so that we might not desire evil as they did. Do not become idolaters as some of them did; as it is written, 'The people sat down to eat and drink, and they rose up to play.' We must not indulge in sexual immorality as some of them did, and twenty-three thousand fell in a single day. We must not put Christ to the test, as some of them did, and were destroyed by serpents. And do not complain as some of them did, and were destroyed by the destroyer. *These things happened to them to serve as an example, and they were written down to instruct us, on whom the ends of the ages have come.* So if you think you are standing, watch out that you do not fall. No testing has overtaken you that is not common to everyone. God is faithful, and he will not let you be tested beyond your strength, but with the testing he will also provide the way out so that you may be able to endure it. (1 Cor. 10.1–13, my italics)

Reflection

Here Paul, who knew his Bible as well as any one, does something that I would never encourage my students to do: namely, assume that a biblical passage speaks solely to them! Like other early Christians Paul wrestled with how his ancestral scriptures related to his new found Way of Jesus Christ. What he does here is not ask what the text originally meant for those to whom it was originally addressed. Rather he tells his Corinthian readers, many of whom as non-Jews probably knew little about the Bible, that this text was meant for them as they lived their life far away from the ancient Israelites in the desert, in the midst of a pagan city centuries later. Like the people in the story they should take heed of this example and learn from it. Here the text of life in pagan Corinth and the text of the Jewish scriptures relate to and inform each other. Paul shows his Corinthian converts how they should 'find guidance for today in the divine message of yesterday'.[10] It is indeed precisely *because* Jews, Christians and Muslims, as in different ways 'people of the book', believe in some sense in an *eternal* message that we have a problem of interpretation at all. After all, if the message was *only* for the time it was written then we do not need to have any relationship to it; but in fact, as John Ruskin says, when 'we take the words of the Bible into our mouths in a congregational way' we 'assert our belief in facts bearing somewhat stringently on ourselves and our daily business'.[11] The Muslim writer Ziauddin Sardar puts the matter in a nutshell: 'I write as every Muslim; as an individual trying to understand what the Qu'ran means to me in the twenty-first century. I believe that every Muslim is duty-bound to accept responsibility for making this effort. I contend that one can only have an interpretative relationship with a text, *particularly when that text is regarded as eternal.*'[12]

One of the first questions to be explicitly asked in Christian biblical interpretation was 'how are the Jewish Scriptures related to the new Christian faith?' A key to the answer given is enshrined in the very words Christians now use for the two parts of the Christian Bible: the 'Old Testament' and the 'New Testament'. We can see the process already in Paul's letters, as the example above demonstrates, but also in his wrestling with how to understand God's relationship to the Jewish people in Romans 9–11. At the Council of Jerusalem reported in Acts 15, the apostles struggled with the meaning of the Jewish scriptures for the new Gentile converts in relation to obedience to the Law of Moses in the light of the their new experiences, not least the increasing numbers of non-Jews included in some nascent Christian communities. The letter to the Hebrews puts the point succinctly about the interpretation of the old in the light of the new, and the new

---

[10]   So Stefan Reif formulates the question for Jews who believe in the eternal message of the Bible. Stefan Reif, 'The Jewish Contribution to Biblical Interpretation', in John Barton (ed.), *The Cambridge Companion to Biblical Interpretation* (Cambridge: Cambridge University Press, 1998), pp. 143–59, at p. 148.

[11]   *Works*, 16, 398–9.

[12]   Ziauddin Sardar, *Reading the Qur'an* (London: Hurst, 2011), p. xv (my italics).

in the light of the old: 'Long ago God spoke to our ancestors in many and various ways by the prophets, but in these last days he has spoken to us by a Son' (1.1–2). Some have interpreted 'old' as 'obsolete', wanting to excise the Hebrew scriptures altogether, as unworthy of the new covenant with God and new understanding of God. The first century theologian Marcion (condemned as a heretic) wished to discard the Jewish scriptures as coming from a lesser deity.

'These things happened to them to serve as an example, and they were written down to instruct us, on whom the ends of the ages have come.' How may a text 'once given' relate to other times, other places and later experiences? The key presenting issue for Paul in our cameo was how might these specific scriptures be used to engage with practices and experiences that were sharp and contemporary for the people he was writing to? The letter to the Corinthians treats of quarrels, sex, food, interpersonal relations, religious worship and death, the core stuff of human lives. The engagement between experience and scripture, in context, is not alien to the biblical tradition but is the very methodology of the Bible itself.

Meta-reflection – or Reflection on the Reflections

Out of my reflection on these cameos I notice four overarching issues, which set the tone and the agenda for our exploration of the Bible and practical theology. They all arise from the dialectic between the text of the Bible and the text of life.

I have begun with people: myself, then my contemporaries, then people further back in time. This is because our lives fundamentally shape the way in which we interpret the Bible, interpret life and seek to relate the two together. Furthermore, in the Bible itself the text of scripture is subordinated to the text of life: life comes first. The shape of this book, therefore, is designed to demonstrate and perform in itself this point.

Second, this text began autobiographically, but opened out to include first others in my immediate communities and beyond that others touched by those others. It then opened further to Christians of the past, and to those of other faiths. I hope that in this opening out it will also invite others in, specifically the readers. Autobiography is not incidental to the interpretation of the text of the Bible or the text of life. Self-reflexiveness, as will be consistently argued, is a crucial method of understanding not only the self, but all that which the self encounters. So the invitation to the reader to engage in their own self-reflection, and the response of the reader to this invitation, are crucial to the performance of the text that is this book.

Third, the Bible is ambiguous. It has been a force for good and a force for evil in history. The relationship between the text itself in this regard and interpretations of the text is disputed and complex. Another way of putting this is to ask whether ideological distortion affects only the interpreters or also the writers/compilers of the Bible.

Finally, context is determinative of how one reads the Bible in relation to life. There is no escape from an effective-history into which we are thrown and within which all our understanding comes about.

Chapter 2
Putting Ourselves in the Picture

All serious uses of theological language are ineluctably 'self-involving.' Or, as a friend of mine once put it, reading the scriptures is an exceedingly dangerous business.[1]

Bultmann and Presuppositionless Exegesis: The Philosophical Context

I was once at a practical theology conference where we were invited to take part in a game. We were all given a set of cards on each of which was written some action: 'take a shower every day', 'drink alcohol', 'commit adultery', 'give to charity', 'vote' and so on. We were instructed to sort them into three piles headed: 'all Christians must', 'no Christian ever should' and 'Christians may choose whether to', and then to discuss our selections with our neighbours. The key point was simple and powerful: we are all deeply embedded in a tradition of belief and ethical practice and we bring some basic presuppositions to the table before we start the discussion. Sometimes we can give a good account of them; sometimes we cannot. Sometimes we have held that view for as long as we can remember; sometimes we are recent converts to it. But we all start from somewhere. We all bring a load of baggage. None of us are presuppositionless.

It was Rudolf Bultmann (1884–1976) who asked: 'Is presuppositionless exegesis possible?' Summing up and advancing the tradition of interpretation in which he stood, he challenged those who would interpret the Bible to see that they came to the text with presuppositions, and that those presuppositions influenced and conditioned their interpretation: 'To understand history is possible only for one who does not stand over against it as a neutral, nonparticipating spectator, but himself stands in history and shares responsibility for it.'[2] Few people would now dispute this, though there are those who virtually discount it in their understanding

[1]   Nicholas Lash, *Easter in Ordinary: Reflections on Human Experience and the Knowledge of God* (London: SCM Press, 1988), p. 243.

[2]   Rudolf Bultmann, 'Is Exegesis Without Presuppositions Possible?', in *Existence and Faith: Shorter Writings of Rudolf Bultmann*, trans. Schubert M. Ogden; reprinted in K. Mueller-Vollmer (ed.), *The Hermeneutics Reader* (New York: Continuum, 1985), pp. 242–7, at p. 246.

of the Bible, while there are others for whom it is explicitly part of their method. The latter include various kinds of self-consciously contextual theologies (as opposed to theology where context is not acknowledged, for *all* theology is contextual). Our presuppositions are not only intellectual beliefs, they are commitments and practices, and they are the places we stand on and from which we view things.

There are several reasons why the explicit recognition of such presuppositions is necessary, and indeed why it is in itself not a liability but a positive asset in interpretation. In the first place, presuppositionless interpretation is impossible. It is vital therefore that we recognise our biases. When Bultmann was accused by his contemporary Karl Barth (1886–1968) of allowing Existentialist philosophy to dominate his reading of the Bible, Bultmann rejoined that at least he admitted to the viewpoint he was coming from and did not therefore have various unidentified philosophical fragments floating in his theological soup: for '"philosophical fragments" float in the soup of all theologians'. To imagine that our reading of scripture is uninfluenced by our presuppositions is to leave those fragments in the soup unidentified, and therefore to risk having a distorted vision of the Bible itself: 'You try to achieve this by ignoring philosophy', wrote Bultmann to Barth. 'The price you pay for this is that of falling prey to an outdated philosophy.'[3]

Furthermore, not to take into account our presuppositions is to ignore our standpoint and therefore to miss the way our perspective conditions the view we have. Such interpretation is defective. If we want to understand what we are seeing and to describe what we see in a way that enables truthful seeing and understanding in ourselves and others, we must take account of and state as clearly as we can the place from where we are looking. It is important to know whether we are seeing an object from in front or behind, for example. This is about perspective, and to understand the perspective of human beings requires, among other things, some analysis of their place within the power structures of society. Do we read the story of the Exodus as Jews or Arabs, the story of Dives and Lazarus as a millionaire or as a homeless person begging on the street?[4]

Finally, our own perspective and self-involvement makes a crucial positive contribution to our act of interpretation. This positive contribution can be compared with the process of counter-transference in psychoanalysis. By analysing our own reactions to the text we learn something about that text from our reactions to it. Of course we also learn something about ourselves, and of course there are factors that complicate and distort our reactions – there is no simple equation – but, just as the psychoanalyst gains insight into their patient through conscious observing

---

[3]   *Karl Barth-Rudolf Bultmann Letters 1922–1966*, ed. Bernd Jaspert, trans. and ed. Geoffrey W. Bromiley (Edinburgh: T&T Clark, 1982), pp. 99, 38.

[4]   See Janet Martin Soskice, 'The Truth Looks Different From Here or on Seeking the Unity of Truth From a Diversity of Perspectives', in H. Regan and A. Torrance (eds), *Christ and Context: The Confrontation between Gospel and Culture* (Edinburgh: T&T Clark, 1993), pp. 43–59.

of their own responses, so we may gain insight into any text by examining what it awakens in us.[5]

Bultmann stands in a line of nineteenth-century German scholars in the humanities who developed a tradition of understanding interpretation that has been deeply influential on work in theological fields ever since. At the head of this line stand Friedrich Schleiermacher (1768–1834) and Wilhelm Dilthey (1833–1911), who developed his work further, in turn influencing Martin Heidegger (1889–1976), thence Bultmann and Hans-Georg Gadamer (1900–2002), and through them, Paul Ricoeur (1913–2005) and the contemporary British theologian Anthony Thiselton (b. 1937).[6] In Chapter 3 we will look at the crucial importance Schleiermacher gives to self-involvement in his account of the human act of interpretation, through his concept of 'psychological' or 'divinatory' moments in the act of understanding. The expectation of self-involvement on the part of the interpreter is a characteristic of Schleiermacher's hermeneutics that is of direct relevance to practical theology, not only to its interpretation of the Bible but in different measure to its interpretation of all texts.

Gadamer and Liberation Theology: The Cultural and Historical Context

In challenging an individualistic view of what understanding and interpretation are, Gadamer is of particular importance to the project of grasping the relationship between the text of life and the written text of the Bible. He insisted that all understanding was historically conditioned. Thus individual self-reflexivity and autobiography are insufficient unless the wider social and historical context is taken into account. Furthermore, his image of two horizons of understanding, the historical horizon of the text and the contemporary horizon of the interpreter, implies an active role for the contemporary interpreter; if the text alone is given the prominent role, the inevitable contribution of the interpreter and their context is ignored and understanding will be only partial: 'examples are oral examinations, or some kinds of conversation between doctor and patient'.[7] This is a good way

---

[5]   For a further development of this theme, see Christopher Rowland, 'The "Interested" Interpreter', in R. Carroll, M. Daniel, David J.A. Clines and Philip R. Davies (eds), *The Bible in Human Society: Essays in Honour of John Rogerson*, Journal for the Study of the Old Testament Supplement Series 200 (Sheffield: Sheffield Academic Press, 1995), pp. 429–44.

[6]   See also Mueller-Vollmer (ed.), *Hermeneutics Reader*; Anthony Thiselton, *The Two Horizons: New Testament Hermeneutics and Philosophical Description with Special Reference to Heidegger, Bultmann, Gadamer, and Wittgenstein* (Grand Rapids, Mich.: Eerdmans; Exeter: Paternoster, 1980); Sally Brown, 'Hermeneutical Theory', in Bonnie J. Miller-McLemore (ed.), *The Wiley-Blackwell Companion to Practical Theology* (Oxford: Wiley-Blackwell, 2011), pp. 112–22.

[7]   Hans-Georg Gadamer, 'The Historicity of Understanding', in Mueller-Vollmer (ed.), *Hermeneutics Reader*, pp. 256–74, at p. 270.

to challenge the concentration of historical critical scholarship on one 'horizon' while it pays lip service to the 'fusion' of horizons, however the analogy of 'conversation' is limited, even misleading, as no text can ever 'speak' other than through the head of the reader and the interpretative tradition of which she is part.

The importance of this radically historicised view of human understanding, which takes into account what practical theology was later to call the 'communal contextual paradigm' and which demands a two-way 'conversation' in order to establish understanding, can be seen in the example of liberation theology.

The growth of liberation theology since the 1960s in Latin America, nourished in a Roman Catholic context by the commitments and statements of Vatican II, and the proliferation of explicitly contextual and advocacy theologies such as feminist and Black theologies, have demonstrated a particular sort of self-involvement in the text of the Bible that is in essential continuity with the position pioneered by Gadamer, though with an explicit socio-political dimension.[8] This involvement is not individualistic but communal, contextual and deeply historically specific in each case, taking rise from a basic question: how may we live as Christians and understand our lives in these circumstances of poverty and oppression? Or as Gustavo Gutiérrez puts it:

> The question we face, therefore, is not so much how to talk of God in a world come of age, but how to proclaim God as Father in an inhuman world? How do we tell the 'non-persons' that they are the sons and daughters of God? These are the key questions for a theology that emerges from Latin America, and doubtless for other parts of the world in similar situations. These were the questions which, in a way, Bartolomé de Las Casas and many others posed in the sixteenth century following their encounter with the indigenous population of America.[9]

Such a question has given birth to the practice of the reading of the Bible by more or less formal base ecclesial communities, a practice in which the lives of the ordinary participants are brought to the text, as the text is illuminated by their lives and in turn informs them, in a mutual and vital dialogue.[10]

In the development of the theology arising from such practices, understanding of the realities of this world is often first mediated through a sociological analysis,

---

[8]   Zoë Bennett and Christopher Rowland, 'Contextual and Advocacy Readings of the Bible', in Paul Ballard and Stephen Holmes (eds), *The Bible in Pastoral Practice: Readings in the Place and Function of Scripture in the Church* (Grand Rapids, Mich.: Eerdmans, 2006), pp. 174–90.

[9]   Gustavo Gutiérrez, 'The Task and Content of Liberation Theology', in Christopher Rowland (ed.) *The Cambridge Companion to Liberation Theology* (Cambridge: Cambridge University Press, 1999), pp. 25–32, at p. 28.

[10]   Christopher Rowland and Mark Corner, *Liberating Exegesis: The Challenge of Liberation Theology to Biblical Studies* (London: SPCK, 1989).

and the results of this analysis are approached from a theological point of view.[11] This process is important, because the vested interests, the positioning in the power structures, whether ecclesial or secular, of those reading scripture and doing theology affect understandings and interpretations, and need to be made explicit and understood. An underlying assumption in liberation theologies is that many dominant theologies in the past, and indeed in the present, have been devised and held by the power-holders, which may ignore or even subvert the interests of the poor and the powerless. So in the context in which liberation theology was born and flourished, self-involvement has to do both with the declared vested interest of the readers and also with the claimed vested interest of other interpreters, which may be hidden.

Self-involvement: Engagement with the Text

In the English language prepositions serve to denote the relationship between one object and another. The prepositions we use to describe our relationship to the Bible are significant. They make explicit what is already existent in the relationship, and using them is a performative act, inviting us to indwell that relationship further. One of the most telling prepositions many people use, one that I was brought up with as a fledgling Christian, is the preposition 'under', used in the expression 'sitting under the text'. This conveys a position of attentive and expectant listening, of learning and of obedience. 'Under the text' is an expression that has carried a whole world of Christian experience particularly in the evangelical tradition, ranging from respect to subservience. It may convey a trustful relationship and loving obedience to God. For many devout readers of the Bible this sense of being guided and taught by God through God's word to us in the Bible has been the mainstay and nourishment of faithful lives. It can, however, have overtones of suppression and restriction of view, which have sadly become realities in some people's lives. But the reality is that 'under the text' in fact means 'under the authority of the interpreters of the text'. After all, texts do *not* speak to us, individuals and communities of interpretation do, and they condition the way in which we understand them. At times what seemed to promise the guidance of God has brought instead all too human instruction, which can end up as manipulation and domination. For some too 'under the text' has implied not fullness of life but a restriction to an inappropriate childishness.

John Ruskin, whom I introduced through a cameo in Chapter 1, was brought up very much in a tradition of sitting 'under the text', almost literally so as he stood as a small child at his mother's knee reciting it and being made to repeat over and over again until his recital was in her eyes perfect. His later story demonstrates both the value of that full and detailed respectful absorption of the Bible, and

---

[11]   Clodovis Boff, *Theology and Praxis: Epistemological Foundations* (Maryknoll, NY: Orbis, 1987).

also the damage from which he sought to escape, of a narrow and confined interpretation and a restrictive style of faith, more frightened to transgress than excited to explore.

In a very different context, the liberation theology tradition brings in a strong sense of attentive listening and determination to act in everyday life, perhaps in costly ways, but subverts the sense of subservience by a commitment to the twin tracks of Bible *and* experience, indeed to the priority of life experience in interpretation. The text is but one ingredient, albeit an important one, in the recipe for life. This method also exposes the Bible to scrutiny and to criticism, as readers allow experience to challenge the text. That does not sit easily with the expectations of 'sitting under the text'.

There are other prepositions that illuminate ways of reflecting our relatedness to the text: over the text, inside the text, outside the text, in front of the text, behind the text, against the text, round and round the text. And then there are the expressions that start with the text rather than with the reader: the text against me/us, the text inside me, the text flowing out of me. Identifying which of these begins to describe our own experience, individual or communal, can be a way in to looking at our personal self-involvement.

'Inside the text' and 'the text inside me' are an interesting complementary pair. They are analogous with the expressions used by Paul in his letters, 'I in Christ' and 'Christ in me'. Such expressions of internalised relationship with the Bible point up several significant issues. First, they point to a way of interpretation that was normal for most Christians in the West until the Enlightenment, and is still normal in many Christian contexts globally. In this way the world is read through the lens of the Bible and its overarching story as taught by the Christian tradition. Christians so indwell the story, and it so indwells them, communally and individually, that it becomes the interpretative framework for life.[12] An emphasis on inhabiting the Christian story, which of course relies heavily on the biblical text, and interpreting our stories through and in the light of biblical stories, and at times the overarching biblical narrative of salvation, is a significant feature of some contemporary developments in the theory and practice of pastoral work.[13]

The mutual indwelling of the Bible – the Bible in me and me in the Bible – has also a deeply personal reference. It points to the intimacy of our relationship with the Bible, often nurtured in devotional reading, remembered from childhood, associated with the deepest events of our lives, sacred to our sense of identity in faith. It was clearly so with Ruskin, and it is on this connection among other phenomena that Schleiermacher is able to build his understanding of psychological

---

[12]   Hans Frei, *The Eclipse of Biblical Narrative: A Study in Eighteenth and Nineteenth Century Hermeneutics* (New Haven and London: Yale University Press, 1974).

[13]   Herbert Anderson and Edward Foley, *Mighty Stories, Dangerous Rituals: Weaving Together the Human and the Divine* (San Francisco: Jossey-Bass, 2001); Charles V. Gerkin, *An Introduction to Pastoral Care* (Nashville: Abingdon Press, 1997); David Lyall, *Integrity of Pastoral Care* (SPCK, London, 2001), especially chapters 3–5.

or divinatory interpretation. But this is not only an individualistic matter; liberation theology illustrates the importance of communal associations and identities in faith and in the reading of the Bible, shared histories that enable shared interpretations. This is *our* story.

Verbs, often linked with prepositions, also carry a wealth of meaning concerning our relationship with the text. Verbs indicate activity – playing with the text, enjoying the text, captured by the text, falling in love with the text, writing on the text, wrestling with the text.

The idea of 'playing with' the text appeals to me hugely. That implies my role as an active interpretative agent. But there is not only that dimension, for it means allowing oneself to be affected by it – a positive way in which one might 'sit under the text' therefore. William Blake (1757–1827) wrote, 'The wisest of the Ancients consider'd what is not too Explicit as the fittest for Instruction, because it rouzes the faculties to act.'[14] So many things are suggested here. This is about the Bible being great enough to match, and indeed tease, the most creative of our imaginings, the wildest of our longings, the furthest stretches of our intellectual and spiritual reach. 'Scripture is like a river again, broad and deep, shallow enough here for the lamb to go wading, but deep enough there for the elephant to swim.'[15] It is a 'classic text' which radically nourishes a whole tradition, the conformists and the prophets within it.[16] Blake's statement also recalls us to that deepest truth of the Bible, which is that in reading it we engage not with the dead letter but with the Spirit of God (2 Cor. 3.17–18), our spirit and God's Spirit within us answering in a living dialogue: 'these things God has revealed to us through the Spirit; for the Spirit searches everything, even the depths of God' (1 Cor. 2.9–16).

'Wrestling with the text' is a much used expression, denoting a sense of struggle – struggle to win through to the meaning, or struggle with the God who is saying difficult things to us in this text. Note the memorable title of John Robinson's book *Wrestling with Romans*, a title to which I have found myself returning imaginatively as I have worked with Ruskin's mid-life diary notes on the text of precisely that letter of Paul's, working at the text, interrogating it, questioning its meaning, returning again and again to wrest some further nuance of understanding.[17] Karl Barth, though an opponent of Schleiermacher's theology in so many ways, echoes his desire to break down the walls between Paul and ourselves, noting in this powerful image in the *Preface* to the commentary on

---

[14]   W. Blake, 'Letter to Trusler', in G. Keynes (ed.), *Blake: Complete Writings* (Oxford: Oxford University Press, 1966), p. 793, quoted in Christopher Rowland, *Blake and the Bible* (New Haven: Yale University Press, 2011), p. 6, which offers a wonderful exploration of Blake's verbal and pictorial 'playing' with the Bible.

[15]   http://www9.georgetown.edu/faculty/jod/texts/moralia1.html (accessed 26.07.2012), St Gregory the Great, Moralia or Commentary on the Blessed Job.

[16]   David Tracy, *The Analogical Imagination: Christian Theology and the Culture of Pluralism* (New York: Crossroad, 1981).

[17]   John Robinson, *Wrestling with Romans* (London: SCM Press, 1979).

Romans: 'how energetically Calvin ... sets himself to rethink the whole material and to wrestle with it, till the walls which separate the sixteenth century from the first become transparent'.[18] This is not just about Calvin; Barth's investment in the very possibility of his own preaching of the Gospel, Sunday by Sunday, drives his reading of the text of Romans: 'I myself know what it means year in year out to mount the steps of the pulpit, conscious of the responsibility to understand and to interpret, and longing to fulfil it; and yet, utterly incapable.'[19]

At first sight it may look as if there are two kinds of issues to be wrestled with: the struggle for understanding of what the text says and the struggle to integrate the text with life, a 'coming to terms' with God's ways. But the two are not really so different. There is no living out that is not embedded in an interpretation, and no interpretation that is not firmly rooted in life and so is conditioned by the life lived. So there is no interpretation of meaning that is not given its colour and contours by the life horizon of the persons or community making the interpretation. This is never clearer than in the radical tradition of Christianity, including liberation theology, in which 'action is the life of all' and in which the direct connection between the biblical text and life lived and political actions taken is most manifest.[20] The connection between understanding and life is, however, also asserted and aimed for in the whole hermeneutical tradition stemming from Schleiermacher.[21]

Conclusions

The philosopher Hegel uses a telling image to get across the centrality of our self-involvement in biblical interpretation: those who study the Bible should not be like so many 'counting house clerks' sitting there counting out other people's money – 'the ledgers and accounts of other people's wealth, a wealth that passes through their hands without their retaining any of it, clerks who act only for others without acquiring any assets of their own'.[22] This is their own money, in which they have a vested interest and to which they are linked with intimate ties. These cover the material, social and communal interests of interpretation, when the readers come to know the text for themselves through

---

[18]   Karl Barth, trans. Edwyn Hoskyns, 'The Preface to the Second Edition', *The Epistle to the Romans* (Oxford: Oxford University Press, 1968; first published 1933), p. 7.

[19]   Barth, 'Preface', p. 9.

[20]   Christopher Rowland, '"I have Writ, I have Acted, I have Peace"', in Zoë Bennett and David Gowler (eds), *Radical Christian Voices and Practice: Essays in Honour of Christopher Rowland* (Oxford: Oxford University Press, 2012), pp. 257–74. For quotation from Winstanley, see T.N. Corns, A. Hughes and D. Loewenstein, (eds), *The Complete Works of Gerrard Winstanley*, 2 vols (Oxford: Oxford University Press, 2009), vol. 2, p. 80.

[21]   See Chapter 3.

[22]   G.W.F. Hegel, *Lectures on the Philosophy of Religion of 1824*, Vol.1: *Introduction and the Concept of Religion*, ed. P.C. Hodgson, trans. R.F. Brown (Berkeley: University of California Press, 1984), p. 128.

involvement with it, and the understanding of human relationships that lie behind our private and public appropriation of the scriptures – all of these illustrate self-involvement and self-investment.

Chapter 3
A Tale of Two Traditions

'He was nervous of us working together with you', confessed my colleague, 'as his kind of practical theology is different from yours; his is more focused on the Bible and doctrine.' This is to put the matter in a nutshell. This chapter addresses two 'traditions' of doing theology. These two traditions, modes, streams, preferences, whatever one calls them, sometimes fight, sometimes cooperate independently, sometimes have an uneasy coexistence. Their practitioners may be more or less self-reflexive about their differences.

One tradition is encapsulated for me in my photographs from my grandson's baptism. Here stands the Vicar by the font in his bright stole, with Mum and Dad and baby. This is the context of the church: its ministers, its sacraments, its buildings, its story and sacred text, its values and its people. Theology may be done within this context, inhabiting trustfully and drawing on all its riches.

The second 'tradition' is focused for me in a photograph from the Occupy London protest, with people outdoors on the street, tents and umbrellas against the rain, placards saying 'the banks own you' and 'this is what democracy looks like'. This signifies to me the outside world, Christians and others mingled, analysis of economics and social structures and political activism. 'Tradition' is not really the right word for this way of being theological and Christian – it is more a kind of sporadic response to opportunity, instances of which have always been present in Christian history. And, as Occupy London has illustrated, Christians have taken up opposing positions in such public matters. We may even want to ask the question, 'why do we need theology here at all?' Cannot and do not Christians cooperate with their fellow human beings in ethical causes on the basis of the analysis of the human sciences, without any necessary recourse to theology?[1]

My two pictures do not represent incompatible realities or even unrelated realities. They are meant rather to act as a heuristic and imaginative device, a way of conjuring up for us very different contexts of action, potentially different priorities and significantly different sources of understanding: different texts and different ways of reading those texts.

---

[1]   See Ivan Petrella, 'The Futures of Liberation Theology', in Zoë Bennett and David Gowler (eds), *Radical Christian Voices and Practice: Essays in Honour of Christopher Rowland* (Oxford: Oxford University Press, 2012), pp. 201–10.

A Route and Some Roots

The route-map for exploration in this chapter is as follows. Having laid out the conception of the two traditions encapsulated in the pictures, I will first address some significant modern historical roots of these traditions in the work of Schleiermacher and Barth. These should be seen for what they are: significant but in no way exhaustive perspectives. Contemporary Roman Catholics, for example, would trace roots and traditions of practical theology and of ecclesial and public engagement in Vatican II and in Catholic Social Teaching.[2] I will then endeavour to identify and analyse differences between these two traditions before moving into more synthetic and constructive mode in exploring how they might work together and be mutually informative while keeping their own distinctiveness. First I will look at Schleiermacher, whose work in hermeneutics is so fundamental for practical theology, and explore his contribution to the discipline. Then I will identify and examine the polarisation between two traditions of theology, encapsulated in the opposition of Barth to Schleiermacher, but representing something with a much longer history, and a continuing one. After examining closely different ways of working with the relationship between theory and practice, I will return to a fuller discussion of the two traditions through the lens of the paired concepts and practices of 'critique' and 'commitment'.

The 'Father of Practical Theology'

Friedrich Daniel Ernst Schleiermacher (1768–1834) is credited with being the 'Father of Practical Theology'. This is usually related to his inclusion of practical theology as a discipline within the curriculum of the Theology Faculty at the new university of Berlin, and to his famous image of a tree with foundational and philosophical theology as the roots, historical and biblical theology as the trunk and practical theology as the branches and the fruit.[3] This inclusion of practical theology, and of the ministerial profession, within the critical scientific endeavour of the new German universities was hugely significant, although the legacy has not been altogether uncontroversial as it has fostered both a clerical/professional/ individualistic approach and a tendency to an applied model in which practice is a deductive 'add on'.[4] There are, however, further and even deeper reasons for the far-reaching importance of Schleiermacher to practical theology.

---

2   James Sweeney, Gemma Simmonds and David Lonsdale (eds), *Keeping Faith in Practice* (London: SCM Press, 2010).

3   Friedrich Schleiermacher, *Brief Outline of Theology as a Field of Study*, translation of the 1811 and 1830 editions, with essays and notes, by Terrence N. Tice (Lewiston, NY: E. Mellen Press, 1990). The image of the tree was not repeated in the 2nd edition (1830) although the arrangement of theology in the tree-like structure remained foundational.

4   For a critique of the 'clerical paradigm', see Edward Farley, *Theologia: The Fragmentation and Unity of Theological Education* (Philadelphia: Fortress Press, 1983), p. 87; and for a counter critique, see Bonnie J. Miller-McLemore, 'The "Clerical Paradigm":

In intellectual and theological history Schleiermacher's work is in part a response to the philosopher Immanuel Kant (1724–1804). Kant's work had undermined the intellectual credibility of the traditional proofs for the existence of God and claimed to have eliminated the possibility of believing in God through reason; 'thereby', he wrote, 'I have found it necessary to deny knowledge in order to make room for faith'.[5] Showing that one could only know things through the five senses and through the manipulation of this data via the innate, structured capacities of the human brain, Kant instituted a 'turn to the subject' in our understanding of how human beings know (epistemology), which left Christians struggling to talk about how God was known. What account can we give after Kant of 'revelation' since it is always we who do the knowing? It is in this context that we need to see Schleiermacher's own 'turn to the subject', that is his assertion that we know God through our 'feeling of an absolute dependence'.[6] While the potential individualism in this is problematic, and counterbalanced by his later contemporary Marx's 'turn to the social', the setting of critical subjectivity at the heart of human knowing is crucial.

There are three central contributions that Schleiermacher's work has made to practical theology. First, he offers a sophisticated account of the practices of interpretation, and of the science of hermeneutics, in a mode oriented to the understanding human subject, which has been deeply influential not only for biblical interpretation but for understanding the act of human understanding in a much wider frame.[7] Second, his exploration of the connections between religious and wider cultural human experience opens the way for an understanding that disciplines beyond the theological are potentially disclosive of fundamental and theological truth. Third, in assigning a role for practical theology within the framework of the theological disciplines he puts on the map in an explicit way the connection between theory and practice in theology.

Hermeneutics: psychological interpretation

Schleiermacher mediated for theology a tradition of hermeneutics that put the interpretative subject at the heart of human understanding and apprehension of truth. His work has been deeply influential, not just for textual interpretation but for practical theological methods as a whole, pointing up clearly as it does the importance of the human and subjective element in interpretation.

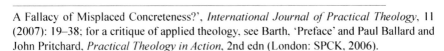

A Fallacy of Misplaced Concreteness?', *International Journal of Practical Theology*, 11 (2007): 19–38; for a critique of applied theology, see Barth, 'Preface' and Paul Ballard and John Pritchard, *Practical Theology in Action*, 2nd edn (London: SPCK, 2006).

[5]   Preface to the Second Edition of the *Critique of Pure Reason*, xxxv. Immanuel Kant, *Critique of Pure Reason*, trans. Norman Kemp Smith, 2nd edn (London: Macmillan, 1933).

[6]   Friedrich Schleiermacher, *The Christian Faith*, trans. M.R. Mackintosh and J.S. Stewart (Edinburgh: T&T Clark, 1928), section 4.

[7]   Friedrich Schleiermacher, *Hermeneutics: The Handwritten Manuscripts*, ed. H. Kimmerle, trans. J. Duke and J. Forstman (Missoula, Mont.: Scholars Press, 1977).

In brief Schleiermacher identifies two kinds of interpretation, both of which he deems necessary. There is the grammatical and comparative moment, which collects the information relevant to the task of understanding, such as lexicographical and grammatical material related to uses by the author and his contemporaries, assessment of linguistic issues, the genre of the literature and biographical information about the author. Then there is the moment he names psychological or divinatory; this is close to what we might call intuitive. What he called the divinatory method requires intuitive perception of, for example, the degree of creativity in the author's style, his leading idea, the author's inner life and the 'way of viewing the world common to both the author and his original audience'.[8] This method, which contributes to a psychological understanding, is deeply self-involving; Schleiermacher describes it as 'understanding the author better than himself' and 'leading the interpreter to transform himself, so to speak, into the author ... gaining an immediate comprehension of the author as an individual'.[9] For Schleiermacher, though not necessarily for those who came after him and built on his work, even the most subjective moments in the interpretative process are inseparable from the objective work. The interpreter must work with both the grammatical and the psychological 'until the two coincide'.[10]

So, this intuitive/divinatory and psychological approach involves the self of the interpreter. 'Divination', Schleiermacher says, 'is aroused by comparison with oneself.'[11] Furthermore, there is a strong claim here that taking account of the reader/interpreter and their life situation helps the act of interpretation. He claims further that the movement is two-way. The movement back from the text to the reader's life situation is as enriching as the movement from the life situation to the text. In other words this act of interpretation includes the act of application not as an add-on but as part of the interpretative moment.

> Even the finest historical reconstruction which we undertake in order to comprehend better a work of some author will achieve true excellence not merely because it clarifies the work in question but also because it enriches our own lives and the lives of others. Such enrichment is sublime, and it should be added to our consideration of works so that we do not produce trivialities which demean ourselves and our scientific labour.[12]

Non-theological disciplines
In the enterprise of theology Schleiermacher valued highly the 'auxiliary' knowledge that came through history and science, as well as through such textual

---

8   Schleiermacher, *Hermeneutics*, p. 79.
9   Schleiermacher, *Hermeneutics*, pp. 64, 150.
10   Schleiermacher, *Hermeneutics*, p. 117.
11   Schleiermacher, *Hermeneutics*, p. 150.
12   Schleiermacher, *Hermeneutics*, p. 207.

disciplines as philology, seeing all knowledge 'im Zusammenhang', 'in the fullness of its relations'.[13]

the undisturbed church

> There are those who can hack away at science with a sword, fence themselves
> in with weapons at hand to withstand the assaults of sound research and behind
> this fence establish as binding a church doctrine that appears to everyone outside
> as an unreal ghost to which they must pay homage if they want to receive a
> proper burial. Those persons might not allow themselves to be disturbed by the
> developments in the realm of science. But we cannot do that and do not want
> that. Therefore, we must make do with history as it develops.[14]

His inclusion of Church Statistics in the 'Historical knowledge of the present condition of Christianity' also indicates an early respect for a sociological approach, 'knowledge of the existing social condition in all the different parts of the Christian Church'.[15]

Schleiermacher did not believe that any one specific revealed, positive historical religion, including the Christian religion, could yield fullness of truth or was free from distortions. He did not on the other hand wish to opt for a universal natural religion, which he considered to be an abstraction and insufficiently rooted in the realities of historical human existence.[16] His overall vision put critically reflexive philosophy as the roots of his diagrammatic methodological tree but required also attention to specific human experiences of God, both within religion and within the wider cultural context. Thus Schleiermacher refused to draw a line between culture and religion, and invited a seeking after truth and a learning to live before God which is affirming and inclusive of human culture, indeed which situates religion within human culture.

While the role of philosophy in relation to theology had been debated for centuries, Schleiermacher in the nineteenth century opens up for us the possibility of taking wider cultural understanding equally seriously as a partner in the theological quest. This significantly involves the possibility of the critique of specific historical religions, Christianity included. Here we see laid out for us a crucial issue in contemporary practical and public theology. Shall we seek for an understanding of God, a revelation, theological disclosure of the truth – of God, of the world and of humanity – through 'positive religion', the authoritative texts of the Christian tradition, or through texts whose origins lie in 'culture', in the secular world and its methodologies? Schleiermacher's orientation to understanding God

---

[13]   See Schleiermacher, *Brief Outline*, p.69 §184 and n. 20.

[14]   Friedrich Schleiermacher, *On the Glaubenslehre: Two Letters to Dr Lücke*, trans. James Duke and Francis Fiorenza (Chico, Calif.: Scholars Press, 1981), p. 60.

[15]   Schleiermacher, *Brief Outline*, p. 71, §195, see also pp. 82–7, §232–50.

[16]   See David E. Klemm, 'Culture, Arts, and Religion', in Jacqueline Mariña (ed.), *The Cambridge Companion to Friedrich Schleiermacher* (Cambridge: Cambridge University Press, 2005), pp. 251–68.

through interpreted human experience led him to a holisitic and inclusive view of the relationship of revealed religion to its surrounding culture: 'Everything human is holy, for everything is divine.'[17]

The tradition of practical theology that flows from him has done likewise, finding iconic expression in Anton Boisen's phrase 'the living human document'.[18] This tradition has embraced human experience and cultural texts in a critically reflexive way, taking a particular post-Enlightenment form. This form includes engagement with the critique of the so-called 'masters of suspicion', Marx, Nietzsche and Freud, and also Darwin, all of whom are with justification regarded as having things to say that are not only not derived from Christian authoritative texts and institutions, but even strongly inimical to them.

Whether such critique as theirs may be appropriated also as internal Christian self-critique, even prophetic critique, is a highly contentious matter, as the example of liberation theology amply demonstrates. The liberation theologian Clodovis Boff, in his magisterial account of the epistemology underlying liberation theology (*Theology and Praxis*, 1987), challenges the then current Roman Catholic view that what he calls 'first theology' can be brought to bear directly onto the experience of people in this world. This, he claims will miss out crucial understandings of this worldly experience, especially those understandings that are laid bare through an analysis of the operation of power. For this we need the tools offered by sociology and other 'this worldly' disciplines. The right process, he suggests, is that raw experience is analysed by means of critical sociological or psychological disciplines, and the *product* of this analysis is subject to scrutiny by theology.[19]

Schleiermacher's third and implicit contribution to practical theology, the opening up of the debate about the relationship between theory and practice in theology, will be best treated at a later stage in this chapter. Before that we turn to a strong and hugely influential reaction to Schleiermacher's way of doing theology in the person and work of Karl Barth.

Reaction: Karl Barth

'One cannot speak of God simply by speaking of man in a loud voice.'[20] The younger Karl Barth's reaction to Schleiermacher encapsulates the other pole in

---

[17]   Friedrich Schleiermacher, *On Religion: Speeches to its Cultured Despisers*, trans. Richard Crouter (Cambridge: Cambridge University Press, 1988; first published 1799), p. 188.

[18]   For Boisen, see Chapter 7.

[19]   For further discussion of this particular method of relating theology, other disciplines and practice, see Zoë Bennett, '"Action is the life of All": The Praxis-based Epistemology of Liberation Theology', in Christopher Rowland (ed.), *The Cambridge Companion to Liberation Theology*, 2nd edn (Cambridge: Cambridge University Press, 2007), pp. 39–54.

[20]   Karl Barth, *The Word of God and the Word of Man*, trans. Douglas Horton (London: Hodder & Stoughton, 1928), pp. 195–6.

my tension, the other tradition of doing theology. The opposition between these two theologians, as explicitly articulated by Barth (1886–1968), has become paradigmatic in a western protestant context.

The dialectical theology of Barth, which emphasised paradox and the 'otherness' of God and the need for a revelation of this divine other, was, like Schleiermacher's very different theology, a response to the questions put on the agenda by Immanuel Kant. Barth's theology changes and develops throughout his long and prolific writing and teaching career, but its fundamental legacy of a belief in a turn back to the God who in autonomy speaks to us and enables us to hear, allied with a suspicion of religiousness and of human culture as a place of revelation, remains strong and deep in his contemporary followers.

As always this must be seen in a historical context, and Barth's attachment to the word of God which stands in opposition to human culture was forged in disgust at the liberal theologians' capitulation to the Kaiser – 'It was like the twilight of the gods when I saw the reaction of Harnack, Herrman, Rade, Euken and company to the new situation'[21] – and later resistance to the German Christians' alignment with the agenda of Hitler. Thus we see immediately that it would be quite wrong automatically to align a stance that *starts* with the Bible with a stance that is *unconcerned* for the world. The Barmen Declaration of 1934 in which Barth was instrumentally involved was crucial for and has become an icon of Christian resistance to evil.

In the recent history of theology the influence of Barth and of Barthian perspectives has been considerable and widespread. In relation to matters touching practical and public theology, direct influence can be seen in neo-orthodox movements, including contemporary explorations of critical realism in practical theology. An example may be found in the work of contemporary practical theologian John Swinton, whose book, co-authored with Harriet Mowat, *Practical Theology and Qualitative Research*, is widely used. In discussing the relative priorities of knowledge derived from theology (revelation) and knowledge derived from qualitative research, the authors specifically invoke Barth and conclude, 'We would suggest that Practical Theology can utilize qualitative research methods to aid in the process of ensuring that Christian practice is in correspondence to the event of God's self-communication.'[22] This is in accord with a basic stance that, 'Within the critical conversation which is Practical Theology, we recognise and accept fully that theology has logical priority; qualitative research tells us nothing about the meaning of life, the nature of God, cross, resurrection or the purpose

---

[21]   Eberhard Busch, *Karl Barth: His Life from Letters and Autobiographical Texts*, trans. John Bowden (London: SCM Press, 1976), p. 81, Letter to W. Spoendlin, 4 January 1915. Ninety-three German intellectuals issued a manifesto identifying themselves with the war policy of the Kaiser when war was declared on 1 August 1914.

[22]   John Swinton and Harriet Mowat, *Practical Theology and Qualitative Research* (London: SCM Press, 2006), pp. 90–91.

of the universe.'[23] Their approach exemplifies well the tradition in practical theology that, while seeing clearly the need for contextual interpretation of God's revelation, finds that revelation as a given and treats it as very much the senior conversation partner.

This has its counterpart in biblical hermeneutics. Anthony Thiselton explores the relationship between biblical material and the present situation. For him they cannot be regarded as fully symmetrical. He puts a test question: 'would it be the same, in principle, to de-centre the present situation as a criterion of theological relevance and truth as to de-centre the biblical texts and their witness to Christ and the cross as a criterion of relevance and truth?' He then seeks to elucidate the lack of symmetry between these two perspectives. At the end of the day, Thiselton's plea is that 'the cross transforms present criteria of relevance: present criteria of relevance do not transform the cross. Salvation is pro-active, not re-active, in relation to the present.'[24] It relativises the determinative power of the present situation and understanding.

This position from a protestant perspective is, of course, not so very far from the position taken by Clodovis Boff above from a Catholic perspective, in which 'first theology' is derived from God's revelation and is the judge of the product of social analysis. This substantiates my suggestion that we need to understand the fluidities and commonalities of different positions within what often feels like a polarisation. It also indicates the natural tenacity within a range of forms of practical theology of the concept of revelation, and this despite practical theology's popular characterisation as experience-centred.

Two Traditions

I do not wish here to explore the historical opposition between Barth and Schleiermacher, but in a rather wider ecumenical context to begin with the place where I work, the Cambridge Theological Federation, where Catholic and Protestant, Anglican and Orthodox, Reformed, Evangelical, Liberal, some from the UK and some international – all rub shoulders as students and staff try to do theology together, learning and teaching on the same courses, worshipping and socialising together.[25] The two traditions, or perhaps better, families of traditions, are similar to those I have found in the wider world of practical theology, but here they are concentrated into a single educational context.

---

[23]   Swinton and Mowat, *Practical Theology*, p. 89.
[24]   Anthony Thiselton, *New Horizons in Hermeneutics: The Theory and Practice of Transforming Bible Reading*, 20th Anniversary Edition (Grand Rapids, Michigan: Zondervan, 2012), pp. 606; 610.
[25]   Zoë Bennett, *Incorrigible Plurality: Teaching Pastoral Theology in an Ecumenical Context*, Contact Pastoral Monograph 14 (Edinburgh: Contact Pastoral Trust, 2004).

We come to the work of practical and public theology bringing with us not only theoretically different perspectives, but, as we see so clearly in the case of Barth, histories that shape us and passions that move us. Tensions may have their roots in powerful and pertinent, but widely differing, historical experiences. For example, in a group looking at the helpfulness or otherwise of Marxian tools of social analysis as part of the practical theological enterprise, an Eastern Orthodox participant said, 'Marxism to you may mean liberation theology; to us it means martyred bishops.' Here history has shaped the communal understanding. As well as this social and ecclesial history the 'history of ideas' is also important: liberation theology and with it the use of Marxian-influenced tools of social analysis grew out of a post-Enlightenment unmasking of taken-for-granted beliefs. We come out of these communal histories, material and intellectual, as well as out of our own personal histories of blessing and abuse, of nurture and discipline, and in such contexts grapple, internally and in dialogue with others, with the tensions created between commitment and critique, between trust and suspicion – suspicion or trust of our own experience, and suspicion or trust of the texts of the tradition, including the Bible.

Over the last 20 years of teaching I have experienced this tension as fundamental to our common life. Time and again, explicitly or implicitly, theoretical stance and practical action are split between a tendency to look to authoritative tradition, in biblical, magisterial or liturgical form, or to look to human experience and humanistic tools of analysis. While our churches often identify three or four sources of Christian understanding and action – for example the Scripture, Tradition, Reason and Experience of the Wesleyan Quadrilateral – in practice the discussion about what is normative for Christian belief and practice often resolves itself into a discussion between two – the Bible/[T]radition and experience. On the one hand, in order to find a way through this polarisation it is imperative to complexify the issue, to see that there are indeed more than two ways of looking at things and that all ways involve interpretation. On the other hand, it is crucial not to avoid or play down the primordial, passionate tension because it is real in the hearts and minds of the protagonists and represents some of their deepest commitments, emotional, intellectual, spiritual and practical.

Three Questions

To tease out this tension further it is helpful to ask some questions. Where do you start? What do you trust? A further question then needs to be developed – what is the relationship you envisage between theory and practice? In this book I am specifically concerned with addressing our use of the Bible, therefore I am looking at the Bible as representative of one pole in this tension. This is not to ignore the fact that this pole might be represented by something else, such as the Church or Liturgy, neither of which is either identical with or completely separate from the Bible.

Where Do You Start?

Anton Boisen enjoined his Clinical Pastoral Education students to learn from the living human documents in the hospital not just the written documents in the library. While all practical and public theologians would want to learn from both, there is a fundamental methodological difference between an idiographic method, which starts with the particulars of lived experience, and a deductive approach, which begins with theory, universal 'laws' and principles, biblical, theological or otherwise, and then applies these to practice. Such a division of approach can be seen in official church documents, in pronouncements of public theologians, in students' dissertations and in individuals' reflections. I am, however, quite convinced that the second approach is by far the most common default mode right across the theological spectrum, whether the 'theory' is the Bible, the Church's tradition, the Liturgy, the pronouncements of theologians or indeed concepts and theories derived from other disciplines.

What Do You Trust?

Behind starting with and giving precedence to the Bible lies a communally handed-down 'tradition' of understanding the Bible's role and of the interpretation of its meaning (differing to a greater or lesser extent in different communities). This tradition has an explicit focus on the revelation of the divine will and on an external authority. Behind starting with experience, on the other hand, lies a preference for the intrinsic authority of the human which though not necessarily originating from the commitments and intentions of the Enlightenment injunction to 'dare to be bold' and to stand up to the authority of Religion has found a natural home in the West in its wake. Another way of starting with experience is the mystical way, which is capable of bypassing extrinsic authority and tradition.

   The positions are evoked powerfully by some of the prepositions and verbs I was playing with in Chapter 2 to describe relationship to the biblical text. 'Under the text' is an expression often used to denote an 'epistemology of obedience'.[26] 'Against the text', on the other hand, is an experience, often painful, of taking a stance that will not let go of primary human experience and interpretations offered of it in the human sciences. 'Playing with the text' suggests a happier mode which knows both freedom and perhaps love; 'wrestling with the text' a darker moment and harder work, but still in mutuality.

---

[26]   Cheryl Bridges-Johns, *Pentecostal Formation: A Pedagogy among the Oppressed*, Journal of Pentecostal Theology Supplement Series 2 (Sheffield: Sheffield Academic Press, 1993), pp. 36, 44.

What is the Relationship between Theory and Practice?

This question, which will be treated more extensively than the first two, returns us to the legacy of Schleiermacher's work. Does the locus of practical theology as the crown of the tree imply a movement from theory to practice, what is often called 'applied theology'? As we consider where we start and what we trust we come up against this fundamental question of the relationship between theory and practice. It is a familiar question across a whole range of academic disciplines, particularly all those that address professional and vocational contexts – for example teaching or music therapy – and those that concern explicitly how we know what we know – for example communication studies or philosophy. It is generally accepted both that experience goes all the way down and also that there is no experience that is not in some way already interpreted experience. So both experience and interpretation of that experience are like lettering in a stick of rock. But this recognition of the importance both of primary experience and of interpretation and 'theorising' still leaves plenty of room for differences in the starting points, trusting places and priorities we hold to. I would like to suggest that there are, in a rough typology that indicates 'ideal types' into which no one fits exclusively or exactly, three ways in which people doing practical and public theology operate. This is useful as a heuristic device but comes with a health warning that it represents 'ideal' and constructed, not real and nuanced, types.

Theory/theology to practice
The first type describes a movement from 'authorised' theology to deduced appropriate practice. The question of the relationship between theory and practice has a particular sharpness when it comes to theology and religion. This is because here we not only have to address the issue of the universal and the particular, which all thinking does, but also are affected by the weight and importance of authoritative tradition and religious belief whose origin is ultimately God.

There are in fact two elements at work here which are mutually reinforcing. To use an everyday image: the well-known glue product Araldite has two tubes – one of glue and one of fixer. It is not till you mix a bit of each together that you get the irreversible hard set. The pull to begin with the theological tradition is so strong because of the mutual reinforcement of two things, which together are immensely powerful. The tube of glue is the desire to prioritise theory, the general rule over the particular, the universal over the single instance. So, we resist the television programme on the National Health Service that argues from a single case of a mother with a sick child rather than a more universal or theoretical analysis. It feels safer to rest on general frameworks than on particular instances, lest we are led astray by the 'tyranny of experience'. The 'fixer' is the authority we vest in the Bible or other elements of the tradition we have received and inhabit. Many of our sources of 'theory' are sacred and deemed to carry divine authority – the Bible, the Magisterium, the Liturgy – therefore they are not considered as open to critique in the way rules and theories might be in other disciplines. This authority works together with the tendency to prioritise starting with theory, 'in the library', and together they bind fast.

This model of moving from theory/theology to practice is typically found in traditions such as evangelical or catholic that emphasise the authority of God mediated through a human channel such as the Bible or the Church. It *may* ultimately be about how much authority is ascribed to God, but it is crucially also about how much credence is given to the demand made upon us of specific mediating texts and institutions, which bring that authority to us. It is also about 'perspicuity' – how clear is the authoritative message – and about how much confidence can be had in the authorised interpreters or mediators of the textual or magisterial tradition to the people. This is often expressed through a theology that ascribes divine presence and legitimation via an understanding of the Holy Spirit's operation in the *correct* reading, and in the activity of divinely sanctioned institutions. There are many strengths in this approach, not least that it avoids merely individual prejudice. As was said to me by a senior church figure, 'I do not believe racism is wrong because I or anyone else experiences it as wrong [after all, others do not experience it as wrong]; I believe it is wrong because the Bible teaches "you are all one in Christ Jesus"' (Gal. 3.28). Such an example immediately shows that you cannot split text and experience easily, as it was on the basis of experience, including the experience of Jesus Christ, that such words were written in the Bible. It does, however, move to a more communal, shared, one might even say 'tested', experience. While this complicates the issue and makes clear that my 'types' are too crude, the point should not be missed that this person's working theology and self-understanding was that his beliefs and actions were to be learned primarily from scripture and then applied in action. One of the primary weaknesses of this position is the difficulty it has in allowing people to cope with new experience, and in particular experience that contradicts what they have been taught, and sets up cognitive, emotional and spiritual dissonance. Above all it prevents people from discerning that which is of God in what seems to contradict received wisdom.

Mutual dialogue between theory/theology and practice
In this second type theology informs practice and what we learn through practice and experience informs theology. This is a mediating position. It is often found actually to dissolve back into something that accords priority in fundamentals to the theology and only a subsidiary role to the practice (as in the positions of both Boff and Swinton mentioned earlier). There is mutual dialogue in which both beliefs and practices are open to change. This model is found commonly in liberation theology, and would be characteristic of much adult theological education in the mainstream churches in the West. Those who hold this position want to forfeit neither the centrality and focus of the Bible and the tradition on the one hand, nor the genuinely disclosive nature of experience on the other. We may learn through experience, they say, indeed we may learn things that change our theology, but we still 'inhabit' the tradition (Tradition) of the Church and

the Bible and this gives us the necessary perspective to read experience. This position entirely accepts the points made in Chapter 1 about coming to nothing without presuppositions. It further embraces the understanding that trustworthy knowledge is mediated through human thinking, and not only thinking but also through human action and feeling.

Opponents of this position who hold type 1 views (above) point out that it opens up the possibility of being led astray by our transient thoughts and feelings which have no real secure basis in any claim to truth and which indeed may lead us away from the truth. Some opponents who hold type 3 views (below) ask on what basis a specific text or institution, whether Bible or Church, can be claimed to have exemption from human ideological distortions. There is potentially a 'tyranny of the text' as well as a 'tyranny of experience'. The Bible was written by humans, mainly men; the canon of scripture was set by the winners; the Church is a human institution, run once again mainly by men and at times deeply corrupted by power – so the argument goes. So how can we accord such texts and institutions a trust that gives them priority in mediating the truth to us?

Practice is all we have
Without claiming access to 'transcendent' or 'authorised' truth, practical theology becomes the exploration of the practices of Christian communities to unearth core values and to bring these into dialogue with the core values of other people and groups. This type is in its explicit form a recent phenomenon. It is laid out classically in its positive aspect in the work of Elaine Graham. In her *Transforming Practice: Pastoral Theology in an Age of Uncertainty* she defines pastoral theology as critical reflection on the practices of the Christian community. This includes not only the community's practices of direct pastoral care but also 'the horizons of value embodied in all intentional practices of faith' including, for example, ethics, worship and education.[27] In principle such an activity may extend beyond the boundaries of the explicitly Christian community to include communities of other faiths or none.

On this model the transcendent or authorised is observed phenomenologically – this or that community is *observed* to believe certain values to be 'given' – and the practical theologian has as a result a certain critical distance. There is, however, a clear sense that the otherness, the alterity, which is experienced when dialogue happens, brings to the process the possibility of questioning from a place that goes beyond, indeed transcends, our starting point. Furthermore, it is impossible to deal with the practices of any community without encountering and engaging with that which those communities regard as authorised. Crucially it is also impossible for the practical theologian to engage in her work without bringing to it her own sense of what is authorised, if only what is authorised by the communities of belief and practice of which she is a part. But there is in this an encounter with 'the other'

---

[27] Elaine L. Graham, *Transforming Practice: Pastoral Theology in an Age of Uncertainty* (London: Mowbray, 1996; reprinted and reissued Eugene, Ore.: Wipf and Stock, 2002), p. 209.

and, if one allows it, the opportunity for one's prejudices to be challenged and new understanding to emerge.

The strength of this position is the possibility it offers of taking the ideological distortions inevitable in human beliefs and practices with deep seriousness. For many people, however, its spirit and orientation is too human-centred, leaving them without recourse to the transcendent God which is so much part of the language of Christian response with its emphasis on obedience to the revelation of God and from God. At first sight it might seem to some critics to fall into Thiselton's category of 'socio-pragmatic' modes of hermeneutics, without access to any place outside of contextual practice from which to critique and challenge practice.[28] However, as noted, a transcendent element is introduced by the openness to the other, to difference, and to comparisons – a process that is precisely the aim and intention of this critical archaeology of practice.

I said that these types were too crude and they are. People do not wholly fit into the one or the other, and people move between them in the course of their lives or as they address different issues. As the critical conversation that is practical theology proceeds, does the Bible (or the Tradition or the magisterial teaching) take precedence or does human experience? Does the Bible or human experience determine the agenda, lead the thinking, have the final say? Where is our first love, our deepest passion, our fiercest loyalty? Where is our heart? Cool analysis may show the nuances; polarisation and passion display the differences.

Critique and Commitment

I initially posed this duality between critique and commitment in order to bring out a contrast between a position that inhabited the received tradition trustfully and a position that more suspiciously critiqued it on the basis of both human experience and secular analyses of that experience. In reverse as it were, one could look at the suspicion in which some hold an appeal to experience or to any 'secular' analysis in contrast to those who trust the wide presence of God in the experiences of human beings and in the analyses produced by human culture. Again, the polarisation is too crude, and in the remainder of this chapter I will look at some ways of nuancing the polarisation and demonstrating how the two 'traditions' or standpoints have elements in common and how they might find common ways of working. I will do this through an examination of theological warrants, of the intertwining of tradition and experience, and of some possible moves of rapprochement.

---

[28]   Thiselton, *New Horizons in Hermeneutics: The Theory and Practice of Transforming Bible Reading*, 20th Anniversary Edition (Grand Rapids, Michigan: Zondervan, 2012), sections xi and xii.

Theological Warrants

The two poles or traditions both have their theological warrants; the question 'what do you trust?' can be pushed back to the question of why and how our trust is warranted. Such warrants have to do with how God and truth are to be understood. The tradition that sits 'under the text' not only locates the revelation of God specifically in the mediation of revelation through the biblical story, and through its authorised interpreters, the 'house of authority', as Edward Farley and Peter Hodgson call it,[29] but crucially also sees the truth of that revelation as guaranteed by a strong doctrine of God's sovereignty – God is able to mediate truth to us and to undergird our understanding of that truth in ways that do not fail. This second theological belief is often missed in the 'softer' versions of doctrines of biblical inspiration, but is fully understood in its more Calvinist origins, of which Van Til's essay mentioned in Chapter 1 is a classic exemplar.[30]

The tradition that would emphasise a freer playing with the text, or even being prepared to take a stance against the text, has different theological roots. The action of the Holy Spirit through the community is believed to have created the text and to have priority over it, and authority of interpretation is seen in quite democratic terms rather than as being invested in particular institutions or persons. Revelation comes not just from the biblical text, and is neither closed by it nor circumscribed by it. Specific understandings of the doctrine of creation as well as of the Spirit underwrite this wider view of the sources of revelation. Theological anthropology also differs between the traditions: the one emphasising the fallibility of human reason and the tendency of the individual human heart to be deceived, the other emphasising the image of God in humankind and also the tendency of institutions to be distorted and of power and authority to corrupt.

Intertwining of Tradition and Experience

Both of these traditions have their roots in experience. While theological warrants are rightly sought and given, it is also fundamentally the case that we adopt our religious beliefs and attitudes in response to our life experiences and the warrants we give are often *post hoc*. So, while it is true that many give warrants based on the Enlightenment 'masters of suspicion' for their critique of Christian traditional views, they have often come to this position through a much more existential kind of 'suspicion' engendered by the abuse they have experienced from church authorities and/or from abuse of the Bible towards them. An interesting public

---

[29]   Edward Farley and Peter Hodgson, 'Scripture and Tradition', in Peter Hodgson and Robert King (eds), *Christian Theology: An Introduction to its Traditions and Tasks* (London: SPCK, 1982), pp. 46–51.

[30]   For an example of the 'softer' version, see John Stott's replies to David Edwards in the dialogue, David L. Edwards with John Stott, *Essentials: A Liberal-Evangelical Dialogue* (London: Hodder & Stoughton, 1988); Van Til, 'Introduction'.

example of this would be Daphne Hampson, whose writings critiquing traditional Christianity draw on precisely these Enlightenment warrants but are also expressly rooted in her own failing struggle to establish her worth and equality as a woman in the struggle for women's ordination: 'To be forced to argue that one is a full human being of equal dignity (for that is what it felt like) is quite extraordinarily undermining.'[31] Likewise, the other tradition, which emphasises commitment and trust, is not just an intellectual one, but grows from a warm stream of living experience. A classic text that inspired and sums up much contemporary conservative evangelical biblical thinking, B.B. Warfield's (1851–1921) *The Inspiration and Authority of the Bible* can be seen to be self-confessedly rooted in the personal experience of God's fatherly love and care in the context of a personal lifestyle of submission to biblical authority. David Kelsey quotes Warfield on how the promises of the Bible were appropriated and experienced though a community of faith, in families and in churches: 'our memory will easily recall those happier days when we stood as a child at our Christian mother's knee' (an issue to which we return when we consider Ruskin on the Bible). 'No other view', writes Kelsey, than the plenary verbal inspiration of scripture 'on the part of the church could make sense [for Warfield] of her numinous experience when she uses it in these various ways'.[32] Experience does indeed go all the way down.

This intertwining of experience and text is rooted in the Bible itself, as was indicated in Chapter 1 in the discussion of 1 Corinthians 10. This takes the form of both the early Christians' reflection on their experience in relation to text found in their scriptures and the presence of 'codified experience' in the text itself – layers of the experience of the community of faith, reflected on, interpreted and written down in their sacred scriptures. This draws out the sense in which whatever we learn of God through the Bible is learnt via the accumulated understanding and handed-down tradition of those who have sought to live and interpret their experience in the light of God. Furthermore there may be a correlation between the interests and practices presented in the text of the Bible and those we experience now. For example, Rosemary Radford Ruether's formulation of the critical principle of feminist theology, 'the promotion of the full humanity of women', is correlated with what she calls the 'prophetic principle', a 'golden thread' of core values which she sees as at the heart of the Bible, running through the Hebrew prophetic books and crucially through the life, ministry and preaching of Jesus. Her appeal to human experience, therefore, is directly correlated with what she finds in the Bible.[33]

---

[31] Daphne Hampson, *Theology and Feminism* (Oxford: Basil Blackwell, 1990), p. 31.

[32] David H. Kelsey, *The Uses of Scripture in Recent Theology* (London: SCM Press, 1975), p. 17, quoting Warfield, *Inspiration and Authority*, p. 107.

[33] Rosemary Radford Ruether, *Sexism and God-talk: Towards a Feminist Theology* (London: SCM Press, 2002; originally published 1983), p. 18, see the whole of chapter 1.

Rapprochement

Thus we see that our understanding and mutual dialogue may be clarified and enhanced both by perceiving the differences between these two poles or traditions and also by realising that the relationship between them is not straightforwardly one of polar opposites but needs to be further nuanced and made complex. A position of critique and suspicion allows one to stand over against the text, taking an outside perspective, perhaps gaining some objectivity by embracing a variety of new views. A position of commitment and trust invites that particular truth of understanding that comes from an insider perspective, and that growth and depth of loving knowledge that comes from trustful inhabiting. Both are needed in a contemporary understanding of the Bible. Three moves may enable a critical dialogue between the two traditions and an overcoming of the polarisation.

Interpretation
Much is gained by moving from the language of 'critique' and 'suspicion' to the language of 'interpretation'. The need for interpretation is something both traditions share. Emphasis on the act of interpretation, and even more, second order reflection on *how* interpretation is done (hermeneutics) achieves two things. It avoids the negative connotations of 'suspicion and critique', which are sometimes invoked by the language of ideological criticism, which suggests some kind of Olympian position that may be impossible for fragile humanity, moving the activity into a realm with more potential for warmth, loyalty and personal commitment. At the same time it indicates the need for even the most 'committed and trusting' approach to acknowledge that all truth is mediated truth and that interpretations differ.

Being critical is a characteristic much prized in a western context as indicating the ability to take a detached and wide view, which in turn is considered to denote maturity of thinking. The priority given to critical reflection can, however, squeeze out other ways of knowing such as the contemplative, the performative, the imaginative and above all the participatory and collaborative. The trustful inhabiting of a tradition of belonging, in which all are recognised and owned, which has been a feature of the lives of religious communities down the centuries, whatever their faults, may give as much if not more insight and wisdom as the ability to stand apart from it with critical distance and suspicion.[34]

Comparison and analogy
Second, the language and processes of comparison and analogy offer new ways of looking at things that are focused positively rather than on suspicion.[35] To lay

---

[34]   Zoë Bennett, Lucia Faltin and Melanie Wright, 'Critical Thinking and International Postgraduate Students', *Discourse*, 3.1 (2003): 63–94.

[35]   Christopher Rowland and Zoë Bennett, '"Action is the Life of All": New Testament Theology and Practical Theology', in C. Rowland and C. Tuckett (eds), *The Nature of New*

two things alongside one another is to invite a fresh viewing of each in the light of the other. This process has been in Christianity from the beginning: the 'old' testament is seen in the light of the new, and vice versa; the experience of the first disciples at Easter is seen in the light of a pre-understanding of 'resurrection' and the understanding of resurrection changed by it; the message of the gospel and contemporary experience are brought into dialogue in Paul's letters. One of the deep concerns of those who operate a 'hermeneutic of suspicion' in respect of received and authorised texts and practices is that such texts and practices should be open to critique and that distortions, abuses and untruths should be 'unmasked'. This may be done through comparisons, through openness to new perspectives and different ways of doing things, which relativise the 'taken for granted'. This mode of relating the text to contemporary reality will be explored in detail in Part II.

Risk

Finally, a willingness to witness and to take risks allows those from one tradition to engage with different commitments and interpretations, and to bring these to bear on their own. This is not easy. To return to Marxism, liberation theology and martyred bishops with which this chapter started: that conversation ended with the words, 'How will you dialogue with us, for whom these things haven't happened?' Listening to what has happened to others but has not happened to us may be a first step in interpretation.[36] That this is difficult and painful is currently made manifest in an acute public way in the Anglican Communion in the 'listening process' associated with same-sex relationships.[37]

Conclusions

I have examined two traditions in practical theology, from a historical and from an analytical point of view. As on the map of biblical hermeneutics I position myself as starting with the reader, so here I place myself on the map of practical theology as committed to starting with the minute particulars of experienced life.

In so doing I do not wish either to undervalue or to obscure the role of theory or of the inherited Christian tradition. There is a story of a young man who asked the older Karl Barth what was the role of reason in his theology; 'I use it', replied Barth. Reason was part of his very modus operandi. Similarly all the traditions that have made us what we are live with us and we with them, consciously or unconsciously. To my attention to the minute particulars of lived experience I bring as well my forty plus years of living in the Christian tradition, and as long of

---

Testament Theology (Oxford: Blackwell, 2006), pp. 186–206.

[36]   See Wendy R. Tyndale, *Protestants in Communist East Germany: In the Storm of the World* (Aldershot: Ashgate, 2010).

[37]   See http://www.anglicancommunion.org/listening/ (accessed 31.07.2012); see also Bennett, *Incorrigible Plurality*.

inhabiting the libraries of Cambridge. And I have, vice versa, always brought my lived experience to these contexts. It may be 'experience all the way down' but it is also 'interpretation all the way down'. All our experience comes to us within an interpretative framework.

Strategies of analogical comparison, emphasis on interpretation rather than critique and recognition that the realities of our practices transcend any neat binary divisions give a starting point to explore the possibilities of working and talking together across 'traditions'. A core thesis of this book is that there are practices and ways of thinking that enable us as practical theologians to avoid sterile polarisations and to live with a more fluid and mobile, a more warm and hospitable, and ultimately a more fruitful and faithful way of engaging with the Bible together.

PART II
John Ruskin: 'To see clearly … is poetry, prophecy, and religion all in one'

The strategy of Part II is to develop an understanding of fruitful practice for the use of the Bible in practical and public theology through the examination of John Ruskin's life and work.

Taking a historical approach of this kind makes two things possible. First it allows us to see how someone in another time and another place brought into dialogue his contemporary context and experience and the text of the Bible. This is a task central to our work as theologians with the Bible. Seeing this diachronically as well as synchronically, from a place and a point of view very different from our own, enables us to have a fresh perspective, bringing new insight and jolting us out of well-trammelled grooves. The historical analogy awakes the imagination and the critical faculties and increases our range of possibilities for understanding the dialectic between the text of life and the text of the Bible. Furthermore, while there are limitations in what can be appropriated from another time and another place in this way, especially in the case of ancient texts such as we have in the Bible, that very process of working with a different historical horizon (in this case the nineteenth century where we have more contextual historical information available to us than is the case with the biblical texts) can illuminate the issue in working between the two horizons of contemporary life and biblical text. This historical method deserves consideration alongside the methods of the social sciences and biblical criticism as a tool available to the practical theologian. While Ruskin is used as a historical hermeneutical dialogue partner to enable a critical perspective, he is also an inspiration, but not a model to follow slavishly. The archaeology of how Ruskin interpreted the Bible is not explored in order to suggest we have the same interpretative strategies as he did, but in order to encourage a similar archaeology of our own strategies to gain some critical purchase on them.

Two levels of analogical comparison are involved here. The first is the analogy between the biblical and the contemporary 'text', both for Ruskin in his day and for us in ours. The second is the analogy between the historical Ruskin in his *'public theology' and our contemporary ways of doing practical and public theology. What is done in this historical comparison is therefore what Clodovis Boff called a 'correspondence of relationships': we look at how the relationship between text of the Bible and 'text' of life in Ruskin might give us a critical handle on text of the Bible and 'text' of life in our own context.*[1]

Ruskin was a reader of multiple texts par excellence. Namely, he read the 'texts' in the world around him, and the text of the Bible was part of his very soul. He knew how to produce his own reflections in the form of written texts which did performative work in the public realm. Above all he knew the importance of good seeing. Accordingly the structure of Part II will follow the pattern of a sustained consideration of John Ruskin: his life, his interpretation of the Bible and, in the final three short chapters, the features of his seeing that make it such an inspiration to the practical theologian.

---

[1]   Boff, *Theology and Praxis*, pp. 142–50.

Chapter 4
'Our national archangel'

'A heavenly book, written by our largely forgotten national archangel', is how Jonathan Glancey in the *Guardian* characterised Ruskin's *Unto this Last*, which 'deserves to be read anew, by all of us, but mostly by ... politicians in search of a moral compass with practical, humane and honest bearings'.[1] He wrote this with reference to the MPs' expenses scandal, but its truth has become increasingly sharp as the financial crisis has deepened; and Glancey is by no means the only person publicly to have invoked the shades of Ruskin in contemporary public life.

The Introduction to this book and Chapter 1 have given a brief anticipatory look at the life and work of John Ruskin, which this next part expands and explores. Glancey is picking up the powerful 'practical, humane and honest' character of Ruskin's social criticism, the content and style of which he believes has much to offer the present day. But here also is a man who has crucial things to offer our consideration of the Bible in practical theology and its use in a public context. His capacity to read a multiplicity of texts and to bring them into critical and creative engagement with one another is outstanding. As an art critic he develops an aesthetic that taps into the deep sources of his biblical understanding, and he penetrates with his imagination the roots of art in the social soul of peoples. As a social critic he includes a condemnation of the ugly in a condemnation of injustice, and he wrestles with the heart of his own biblical faith to find the place of justice in it. As a man of faith he reads the Bible every day, seeing the landscape painting of Turner as the manifestation of God's being and glory, the abject poverty of rural Switzerland or industrialised Britain as the darkness of godlessness. He writes the list of the Companions of the Guild of St George on the pages of his Bible; he writes notes on the interpretation of Paul's letter to the Romans on the pages of his diary which also includes drawings of flowers and rocks. His hermeneutic of the Bible is intimately connected to the fact that he is a reader of multiple texts, and is fundamentally linked to his capacity to relate them to one another.

Ruskin models for us a critical subjectivity in respect of the Bible. He is conscious of his own reading history, of how his understanding of the Bible has developed. This applies to phrases in particular verses as he observes his understanding change from year to year, and to his grasp of the place of the Bible as a whole in his view of the meaning of human life and of religion. He is self-

---

[1]   Jonathan Glancey, 'Of Skeletons and Souls', *The Guardian*, 19 June 2009, p. 35.

reflexive. His method is also, as I have stressed in Chapter 1, self-involving. He believes in loving not dissecting: 'All true science begins in the love, not the dissection, of your fellow creatures; and it ends in the love, not the analysis, of God.'[2] In this same spirit he commits himself to the biblical text and to what he believes it means through his wrestling with it. The Bible is not someone else's coinage, but the stuff of his own life. From this insider perspective he is able to be critical. He protests as well as praises; he disowns as well as owns.

Seeing is crucial to the discipline of practical theology, where attention to 'seeing, judging, acting' has been fundamental to its practice. Ruskin's capacity to 'read' a multiplicity of texts was sustained by his ability to look at, to see and to interpret a multiplicity of objects, whether written texts, images or buildings. How he did so, and how he then produced the fruits of this reflection in a life and in works that had huge influence in the public square, offers a unique insight into the approach to what an appropriate public theology might be, for to '*tell* what it saw' is as important to Ruskin as to see clearly: 'the greatest thing a human soul ever does in this world is to *see* something, and tell what it saw in a plain way'.[3]

Discussion of Ruskin's work can furnish us with a fresh perspective on practical theology and theological reflection. His knowledge of the Bible enables us to discern how a biblically informed engagement might work, in ways that are as good as, and in some ways probably better than, many contemporary examples. One may see Ruskin's work as a resource that has its own context in which it has to be understood and that can, through mutual critique of text and text and of text and context, offer guidelines for a contemporary public theological engagement.

The hermeneutical move I want to make in using a historical figure in this way can be beautifully illustrated from John Ruskin's own home, Brantwood. Among the extensive gardens there is a small slope known as the Zig-Zaggy Garden. This is a reconstruction of a garden Ruskin used to have, modelled on Dante's Purgatorial Mount, with ascending sections vividly portraying the seven deadly sins. Ruskin's garden is long since gone. The guide who took me round explained that the reconstruction had been determined by three factors: a written letter from Ruskin to his cousin containing two tiny sketches which describe his garden, traces of the original garden found on the site and a new interpretation of this material by a contemporary South African horticulturalist. She was asked to create a new garden which would attempt to do for twenty-first-century viewers what Ruskin's had done for his own time.

In this book I want to use an analogous process by creating a 'Zig-Zaggy garden' in the guise of something like an interpretative inspiration for engaging with the Bible, and for using it in twenty-first-century Christian public life. To call this a model would be to distort what I am doing; Ruskin is much more an inspiration for me and for this book than he is a model. To pick up the Zig-Zaggy garden analogy, what I am doing is seeking to understand his use of the Bible

---

2   *Works*, 26, 265–6.
3   *Works*, 5, 333.

through his own writing, and through traces he has left behind, and thence to create
something new which can inform and inspire in the twenty-first century. There is
a sense in which this is in part an exercise in Reception History, an approach
to interpretation of the Bible through exploring how it has been received and
used throughout history, how it has been interpreted, what impact it has had and
what further acts of creativity it has inspired, but it is not only a merely historical
exercise but a hermeneutical and pedagogical one too.[4]

Part II explores in detail those characteristics of John Ruskin's seeing, reading
and proclaiming that may act as an inspiration and a critical model for contemporary
practice. It is first necessary to explore something of the man himself; Ruskin's
context and his life are essential ingredients for the understanding of his use of
the Bible, as they are indeed for everyone, a fact that is insufficiently recognised.

John Ruskin: The Man and his Life[5]

John Ruskin was born in 1819, the only son of John James Ruskin, sherry
merchant, and Margaret Ruskin, at whose knee he daily learned to recite the Bible
chapter by chapter. His parents were devoted to him, and believed deeply that he
had special gifts to offer. He lived in the family homes in South London (Herne
Hill and Denmark Hill); at Oxford, both as an undergraduate when his mother took
lodgings in the High Street and he took tea with her each day, and later as Slade
professor of Fine Art (1869–79, 1883–85); and at Brantwood, by Lake Coniston
in Cumbria, a house that he bought in 1871 with money inherited from his father
who had died in 1864.[6] Ruskin never had to work to earn his living. He travelled
extensively, in a private horse-drawn coach, initially with his parents, both in the
UK and in Europe, learning to love the beauty both of the natural scenery he
visited, especially the Alps, and of the architecture and the art he saw. Married
once, unhappily, Ruskin remained single for the remainder of his life, for much
of it deeply and painfully in love with a young Irish woman nearly thirty years
younger than himself, Rose La Touche, who died in 1875 at the age of 27.

Some of the key works Ruskin wrote are *Modern Painters* in five volumes
(1843–60), *Stones of Venice* (1851–53), *Unto This Last* (1860, 1862), *Fors*

---

[4]   Zoë Bennett, 'Ruskin, the Bible and the Death of Rose La Touche: A "torn
manuscript of the human soul"', in Michael Lieb, Emma Mason, Jonathan Roberts and
Christopher Rowland (eds), *The Oxford Handbook of Reception History of the Bible*
(Oxford: Oxford University Press, 2011), pp. 576–89.

[5]   The definitive biography of John Ruskin is Tim Hilton's *John Ruskin* (New Haven
and London: Yale University Press, 2002). Excellent material can also be found on The
Victorian Web at http://www.victorianweb.org/authors/ruskin/index.html and on the
website of the Ruskin Library and Research Centre at Lancaster University at http://www.
lancs.ac.uk/users/ruskinlib/ (both accessed 23.07.2012).

[6]   http://www.brantwood.org.uk/ (accessed 24.07.2012).

Clavigera: Letters to the Workmen and Labourers of Great Britain (1871–84)
and finally *Praeterita* – his autobiography (1885–89). *Modern Painters*, the first
volume of which was published when Ruskin was 24, began in an impassioned
plea for the superiority of the virtues of the contemporary artist J.M.W. Turner
(1775–1851) and worked through much of the painting of Europe, presenting
advanced aesthetic theory, which changed and developed. Robert Hewison makes
a strong case for the rootedness of Ruskin's aesthetic understanding in his early
evangelical heritage with its typological interpretation of the Bible.[7] His early
interest in painting was specifically in landscape. *Stones of Venice* marks Ruskin's
growing understanding, demonstrated also in the later volumes of *Modern
Painters*, of the connections between art and human society. The publication of
Unto this Last in *Cornhill Magazine* in 1860 signals Ruskin's definitive 'turn to
the human' in his public writing and also his turn from the more golden prose and
long flowing sentences (some of the best ever written in the English language
and much influenced by the language of the King James version of the Bible) to
the pithier more sermonic form of short essays and later letters. *Fors Clavigera:
Letters to the Workmen and Labourers of Great Britain* is an extraordinary work.
Archbishop, later Cardinal, Manning described it in a letter to Ruskin in October
1873 as 'like the beating of one's heart in a nightmare'.[8] In public letters over 13
years, somewhat like a newspaper columnist, Ruskin poured out his soul, with
frightening clarity of insight and with occasionally disturbing glimpses of his rising
insanity, concerning the state of the nation. The work is peppered with biblical
quotations and allusion, no longer rooted so much in a typological reading but in
an immediacy of analogy and prophetic urgency. *Praeterita* – his autobiography –
is his mature work of reflection, and a good place to start reading Ruskin.[9]

Practicality was not Ruskin's greatest gift; nevertheless he cared very much to
put his ideas into practice. He founded a museum, a teashop and a cottage lace-
making project; he acquired and worked land; he set up a project for road digging
and one for road sweeping. He concerned himself and his financial resources with
housing, education, working and commercial practices. His grand project was the
Guild of St George, which was

> conceived as a utopian social mission whose plan, though never fully realized,
> was to put into practice Ruskin's commitment to just economic and social
> relations. It was an institutional expression of faith in moral reform. It was both
> an attempt to ameliorate the worst effects of modern capitalism, and to return to

---

[7]   Robert Hewison, *John Ruskin: The Argument of the Eye* (London: Thames &
Hudson, 1976). See also George Landow, *Victorian Types, Victorian Shadows* (Boston,
London and Henley: Routledge & Kegan Paul, 1980).

[8]   *Works*, 36, lxxxvi.

[9]   Available at a very modest price in a 2012 paperback edition, also on Amazon
Kindle, edited by Francis O'Gorman in the Oxford World Classics series.

a pre-capitalist model of society that Ruskin believed was free of exploitation, just as it was free of mechanized industry.[10]

The Guild of St George is still in existence.[11] None of Ruskin's projects ever worked on a larger scale or on a long time frame in the form in which he initiated them, however endeavours on which he had a long-term influence include the Arts and Crafts Movement, the National Trust, Toynbee Hall, the Workers Educational Association and the founding of the Labour Party in Britain. Much of this was through the immense inspiration, and practical support, he offered to others.

Religiously speaking, Ruskin was brought up an evangelical. As an adult he found his evangelical inheritance increasing difficult to relate to his mature self, and in 1858 experienced a form of 'unconversion' or turning away from his old form of faith. He describes this himself in three different accounts, two retrospective.[12] This was certainly an unconversion from the evangelical piety and exclusivism that was represented so totally for Ruskin in the figure of the preacher in the service near Turin which so turned him 'off' – a 'squeaking little idiot', a 'poor little wretch in a tidy black tie', a 'somewhat stunted figure in a plain coat with a cracked voice' – you can feel his underlying emotion – but it was not a total unconversion from Christianity.[13] With a growing ecumenical inclusiveness of other Christian and non-Christian perspectives, including an interest in ancient mythology, Ruskin embraced what he called a 'religion of Humanity' which, however, continued to be deeply informed by his ongoing daily reading of the Bible.[14] Around 1875 he returned to a less evangelical Christian understanding – one that could be very critical of the church and its leaders.

From 1878 onwards Ruskin suffered a series of debilitating bouts of mental illness, culminating in his final years of virtual silence. He was cared for at Brantwood by his cousin Joan Severn. His interest in and philanthropy towards the local people, including the school, are delightfully recorded in a leaflet at the Ruskin Museum in Coniston, in the words of a local schoolboy: 'He's a foony man is Meester Rooskin, but 'e likes us to tak a good tea.' Ruskin refused burial in Westminster Abbey, and lies instead in Coniston churchyard, among his family, friends and servants. His grave is surmounted by a north-country Saxon cross, designed by his biographer and personal secretary, 'cut from the stone of the dale

---

[10]   Stuart Eagles, *After Ruskin: The Social and Political Legacies of a Victorian Prophet 1870–1920*, Oxford Historical Monographs (Oxford: Oxford University Press, 2011), p. 52.

[11]   www.guildofstgeorge.org.uk (accessed 25.07.2012).

[12]   See *Works*, 7, xli; *Works*, 29, 89; *Works*, 35, 495–6.

[13]   See Chapter 5, pp. 69–70.

[14]   *Works*, 29, 90.

where he made his home, carved by a local sculptor ... with allusions to his life's work and signs of the faith in which he died'.[15]

Ruskin's life was virtually coterminous with that of Queen Victoria (1819–1901; reigned 1837–1901). Charles Darwin published *On the Origin of Species* in 1859; Charles Lyell had published *The Principles of Geology* in 1830–33; and Ruskin, an amateur geologist in his youth, was deeply affected by the questions posed to Christianity by these advances in scientific understanding – 'If only the Geologists would let me alone, I could do very well, but those dreadful Hammers! I hear the clink of them at the end of every cadence of the Bible verses.'[16] In 1846 George Eliot translated Strauss's *The Life of Jesus Critically Examined*, and in 1854 Feuerbach's *The Essence of Christianity*, bringing German 'Higher Criticism' of the Bible into English intellectual life. Ruskin himself became embroiled in the defence of Bishop Colenso in the 1860s as Colenso's daughter attended Winnington School in Cheshire where Ruskin was a benefactor and regular visitor. He wrote of his long, lonely struggle with the Bible, 'And the solitude was terrible ... But now the Bishop has spoken, there will be fair war directly, and one must take one's side, and I stand with the Bishop and am at ease.'[17] An acquaintance of both F.D. Maurice and C.H. Spurgeon, Ruskin shared more in common theologically with the former but found the latter better company: 'nightly, at Spurgeon's tiny south London house, tasting wines from John James's [Ruskin's father's] own cellar, Spurgeon with a cigar, they would spar over their intimacy with Scripture and their utterly different natures, Ruskin provocative, Spurgeon laughing at him, each capping the other'.[18]

Ruskin knew Gladstone personally – he visited him at Hawarden and corresponded with his daughter, Mary. Though he was a natural Tory – he opens his autobiography 'I am, and my father was before me, a violent Tory of the old school; – Walter Scott's school, that is to say, and Homer's',[19] party politics scarcely interested him. In reading Ruskin's work one gets little sense of the intricacies of political debates and personalities, but a strong and vivid sense of the social and economic situation of industrialised capitalist Victorian Britain, and the ravages of poverty, ill-health and a polluted environment. Foreign policy, imperial or European, interested him less, although wars and peace in Europe affected both Ruskin family travel and more generally the opening up of the art treasures of Europe to British (and Ruskin's) scrutiny.

---

[15]   W.G. Collingwood, *The Ruskin Cross at Coniston* (Ulverston: W. Holmes, 1910; reprinted and published Coniston: M.J. Salts, January 2000), p. 4.

[16]   *Works*, 36, 115.

[17]   *Works*, 36, 425.

[18]   Hilton, *John Ruskin*, p. 261, and see also p. 262 for contrast with Ruskin's relationship with Maurice.

[19]   *Works*, 35, 13.

Ruskin the 'Public Theologian'

John Ruskin is not often thought of as a 'public theologian'. He was, however, a man who was able to do the very thing he valued so highly in others: he was able to see clearly and to tell what he saw in a plain way. He worked with the Bible in such a way that it was able, in Schleiermacher's words quoted in Chapter 3, to enrich his own live and the lives of others. The sheer quantity of biblical references in Ruskin's work alerts us to the functioning of a biblically-formed sensibility, moral and aesthetic. Ruskin read the Bible daily throughout his life. This began with his childhood daily recitations of the Bible, two or three chapters a day, beginning with Genesis and going through unremittingly to Revelation and beginning the next day with Genesis again. So his mother bestowed on him 'the most precious, and, on the whole, the one *essential* part of all my education' and by this process 'established my soul in life' and 'gave me secure *ground* for all future life, practical or spiritual'.[20] It continued through his childhood and adolescent reading and writing of sermons, detailed notes of wrestling with the Bible in personal diaries and annotations on medieval biblical manuscripts which he used (in Greek) for his daily reading. His public lectures, letters, books and essays are replete with Bible quotations and allusions. His close engagement with the Bible persisted through all phases of his faith. In 1898 Mary and Ellen Gibbs produced a 300-page volume of the biblical quotations in what had thus far been published of Ruskin's work. Immediately after his death in 1901 one of the first tributes to him, a French work by H.J. Brunhes, was entitled *Ruskin et la Bible.*[21]

The extent of Ruskin's influence is generally acknowledged. *Unto this Last* was held in great admiration by the early leaders of the Labour Party, who in a survey in 1906 of authors and books that had influenced them mentioned Ruskin most frequently; by Mahatma Gandhi who claimed in his autobiography that it had changed his life and converted him to the importance of home industry and craft work; and by Martin Luther King whose case of personal effects on display at the King Center in Atlanta Georgia includes an Indian copy of the book.[22] In Gandhi's words about him, 'A poet is one who can call forth the good latent in the human breast.'[23]

---

[20]   *Works*, 35, 42–3.

[21]   H.J. Brunhes, *Ruskin et la Bible* (Paris: Perrin, 1901); M. and E. Gibbs (arr.), *The Bible References in the Works of John Ruskin* (London: George Allen, 1898). See also Zoë Bennett, '"There is no other light than this by which they can see one another's faces and live": John Ruskin and the Bible', in Neil Messer and Angus Paddison (eds), *The Bible: Culture, Community and Society* (Edinburgh: T&T Clark International, in press).

[22]   For Ruskin's influence on the early Labour movement, see Eagles, *After Ruskin,* chapter 5.

[23]   http://www.nalanda.nitc.ac.in/resources/english/etext-project/biography/gandhi/part4.chapter18.html (accessed 25.07.2012).

The biblical formation, however, of such an influential social critique is largely underplayed. Although it is alluded to it is not given the substantial place it deserves in understanding the generation of Ruskin's ideas and commitments. In his fascinating recent book *After Ruskin*, Stuart Eagles explores the influence of Ruskin's social and political views on British social activists between 1870 and 1920. In attending to what influenced Ruskin's own thinking and action he mentions several sources: Plato and Xenophon, Wordsworth and Coleridge, Gothic architecture and medieval Venice, his own Scottish heritage and Walter Scott's Toryism and romantic version of medieval society, his intellectual rootedness in art history and criticism. Eagles does not include the Bible; yet even a cursory reading of *Unto this Last* makes plain the debt to Ruskin's biblical upbringing and daily attention to the text of the Bible.[24]

Ruskin displays a range of attributes that we would expect of a public theologian, although I do not claim for a moment that he names himself as such. The Bible is not the only element of the Christian heritage on which he draws: the painting and architecture of Christian Europe are a rich source of inspiration. He sees stories in stone – from the wide sweep of Venetian history depicted in its architecture, to the details of the sculptures on Amiens Cathedral. His title *The Bible of Amiens* conveys this vision. Or he reads stories in painting – so aptly put in his autobiography of the Campo Santo in Pisa: 'the entire doctrine of Christianity, painted so a child could understand it'.[25] I mention briefly here the range of characteristics of Ruskin's work that make him an excellent example of what we look for in a public theologian, characteristics that are explored in much more detail in Chapter 9. These are that his work is rooted in the contemporary world, is both personal and public, draws on the Christian heritage and its traditions, is carefully and creatively crafted, and is performative – to encourage action, to bring healing or understanding, or to enable growth, personal or communal. Ruskin's self-understanding, reflected in his public use of the Bible, is that he was not using it as 'a foundation of religious concrete, on which to build piers of policy' but was appealing to a commonly held set of public values, biblically rooted but drawing on a non-exclusive approach to the Bible, in order to shame and galvanise his fellow citizens into action for social change.[26]

Conclusions

In his lifetime and since his death various groups and individuals have picked up Ruskin's work and run with the inspiration it engenders – in education, ecology, economics, politics, housing, arts and crafts. This continues to be the case

---

[24]   Eagles, *After Ruskin*, pp. 30–31.
[25]   *Works*, 35, 351.
[26]   *Works*, 17, 348.

today.[27] Ruskin never wanted there to be 'Ruskinians'. He wanted to inspire and teach people, not to produce uncritical imitators or idolaters: 'no *true* disciple of mine will ever be a "Ruskinian"'! – he will follow, not me, but the instincts of his own soul, and the guidance of its Creator'.[28] As the following chapters of this section look deeply into that which Ruskin most prized, the art of seeing – seeing clearly, seeing with the heart and seeing prophetically – it is a matter of inspiration not of slavish imitation.

In John Ruskin we have a 'national treasure', whose practical and honest humanity has much to teach our current generation. We have a man whose biblical faith informed his political analysis and his social protest. His public writings and private wrestlings with the Bible are an invitation to the practical and public theologian to enter his story and to make of it for theology, as well as is done for other public practices, our own Zig-Zaggy garden, fit for the purpose of inspiring contemporary public theology.

---

[27] For example, the work of the Ruskin Mill Trust, whose purpose is, 'To advance the education of young people with learning difficulties and/or behavioural problems or special educational needs through training in the areas of arts, crafts, agriculture and environmental sciences'. See http://rmt.org/our_vision_and_values (accessed 30.04.12).

[28] *Works*, 24, 371.

Chapter 5
Ruskin's Biblical Interpretation

Life and Text

It is impossible to separate someone's biography from the interpretative categories they use, their life story from the way they read and understand the Bible. This chapter, therefore, is in direct continuity with the last biographical chapter, and what has been learned of Ruskin thus far is integral to understanding how Ruskin interpreted and used the Bible in his acute and insightful perceptions of his contemporary world, and in the public texts through which he commented on that world and hoped to spur his fellow human beings into transformative action.

To sum up where we have got to thus far: Ruskin learned the Bible, indeed effectively learned both to read and to write, by reciting chapters daily to his mother; the Bible continued to be a source of meaning and inspiration to him throughout his life, and for much of this he read it daily, often in the Greek text, in manuscript form. His understanding of the nature of the Bible changed as his understanding of Christianity and its place in the world changed; his apprehension of how we know God became enlarged and more free-ranging as he grew older and integrated his apprehension of beauty with his appreciation of the Bible as the word of God. His relationship to the Bible was shaped in response and reaction to two of the most significant relationships of his life: with his mother and with the woman he loved. This relationship to the Bible was deeply personal, its intimacy bringing both warmth, on the one hand, and boldness of criticism on the other. The Bible was a crucial influence and a continually wielded weapon in his public fight against injustice.

'[A]t all times he took the Bible seriously, and in many a passage he has made its thoughts and stories live for us with marvellous reality.'[1] So wrote William Gershom Collingwood, disciple of Ruskin from Oxford days, personal secretary and lifelong friend. Furthermore, believed Collingwood, Ruskin's mind can be read and understood in the annotations he made on his Bibles: 'anyone who wishes to follow Ruskin in his more intimate thoughts on the Bible, at the time of crisis in 1875 ... anyone who wants to get at his mind would find it here'.[2] 'Here' is in a certain set of Greek manuscripts, and 'here' was where my own quest began. It

---

[1]   W.G. Collingwood, *Ruskin's Relics* (London: Isbister, 1903), p. 195.
[2]   Collingwood, *Relics*, p. 202.

was at first a quest for an understanding of Ruskin, but as time went on my own longer and deeper quest, for understanding of the Bible itself, merged both with the stream of Ruskin's quest for this very same thing and also with my quest for understanding of that quest of his.

As I read Collingwood's book in the library in Brantwood, overlooking the Coniston lake and fells, there began a journey for me: to find these Bibles and to get to know the man John Ruskin. The first Bible in the British Library proved to be a treasure – a medieval manuscript Gospel Lectionary annotated at the foot of every page, in ink, by Ruskin in his daily Bible reading, just as Collingwood had said.[3] That has proved to be a longer journey than I first imagined. It has not only been a research journey, but a personal journey. The knowledge of a historical figure has been, as Schleiermacher would have said, enriching of my own life, and has shaped and coloured the story of my relationship with and interpretation and use of the Bible. This is entirely in keeping with the 'readerly' orientation of my hermeneutics. My life has been affected by the texts and traces of Ruskin, as both of ours have been affected by the Bible. It is in the hope that such an intertwined set of stories is sufficiently open-textured to invite into it also the stories of others that I write this book.

Ruskin's Strategies of Interpretation: Commitments and Ways of Reading

Ruskin's personal reading history, and the development of his own understanding, deeply interested him. He reflects in his diary in 1858 concerning the interpretation of 'man does not live by bread alone' in the temptation story and of the connection with the feeding with manna: 'I can understand nothing. Still less can I understand what particular points I was thinking of when I wrote that', and again in further notes in 1859, 'I suppose this was the way I lost understanding of the words before.'[4] Similarly in the lectionary annotations he constantly alludes to the state of his comprehension – 'After a life's thinking I have not the least idea what this passage means or what a *skandalon* is.'[5] While these things he has *not* understood need to be set against the fresh and intriguing discoveries and explanations with which his notes brim over – from detailed comments on translation of the Greek to idiosyncratic personal reactions – what such comments reveal is not only self-reflectiveness but an astonishing level of tolerance of doubt and uncertainty. He recognises that as a reader he is engaged in a process over time, and a process that is not and never will be shaped by perfect understanding. He is not haunted by a need to be right.

---

3   British Library, Egerton 3046, Evangelistarium.

4   Unpublished diaries for 1858/1859: RF MS 11, Ruskin Foundation (Ruskin Library, Lancaster University), folios 32, 107.

5   Egerton 3046, 95R, reference to Luke 17.1–5.

He is always asking questions of the text – why is this included? What does that mean? He does not mind if he doesn't get an answer. In one of his Sunday letters to the girls of Winnington School he says that they are to be

> quite clear in all your reading – & especially Bible reading, whether you really understand or not. Few people have the good sense to be vitally and thoroughly puzzled. They read all in a mist; and never come to a positive stop.[6]

And to Margaret Bell, the headmistress, he writes:

> [M]y very first principle in Bible reading is neither to want to *bring* out anything – nor to be *afraid* of *finding* out anything; and only to make sure that whatever I read, I either *do* – or *don't* understand … all depends on taking [the words] precisely in their accurate & entire meaning: then, if we understand them on these terms, all is well; if, on those terms they appear inexplicable, mark the text as a short one – clearly – with the chalk – 'That's a locked door' – Well, it would be odd if all doors were open at once – go on to another, and we shall perhaps find that one open when we come back.[7]

Certain features of Ruskin's biblical hermeneutic are sustained throughout his adult life. In particular, his commitment to justice and servanthood as the heart of the gospel, to the call for practical obedience as a central thrust of the biblical message and to a preference for those elements of the biblical message that are firmly rooted in *this* world and its realities are displayed throughout both his public and private comments on and use of the Bible. From his reading of *dikaiosune* as justice rather than righteousness, a word he feels in English 'has … prevented most persons from feeling the force of the passage in which it occurs', to his noting that the New Testament is from start to finish about actions, Ruskin expounds the Bible as a book that teaches us how to live well with one another under God.[8]

> You have – in the beginning of the New Testament – and at the end of it: – two great teachings about the Kingdom, Both by Christ … The first words are Matt. 5th.3 – the last, Rev.22nd 14-17, – giving (taken together:) – the full blessing – first the subduing of the heart to obedience – then the fulfillment of obedience – then the Reward of obedience … obedience by *action* … When first however you begin to see how throughout the Bible Deeds are the test, and not words nor Creeds, – there comes a terrible feeling over some minds as if they could never do enough… . [But] … [a]s soon as people begin to work for Christ really – they

---

[6]   V.A. Burd, *The Winnington Letters: John Ruskin's Correspondence with Margaret Alexis Bell and the Children at Winnington Hall* (Cambridge, Mass.: Belknap Press of Harvard University Press, 1969), p. 194.

[7]   Burd, *Winnington Letters*, p. 156.

[8]   *Works*, 17, 59; and diary notes on Romans.

find it just like working for their father in his garden. They never need to be afraid of not doing enough to please him – sometimes they may not do quite as much as they should – but all that He'll say will be, 'Well – my dear, I think you might have dug a little further this morning – but never mind – go & get your dinner - and I'll do this bit for you.'[9]

Such 'digging' is a following of Jesus: Ruskin considers Luke 22.24–7, which culminates in Jesus saying 'I am among you as one who serves', 'one of the most important in N.T.'.[10] He is interested in orthopraxy rather than orthodoxy. Furthermore, Ruskin's biblical interpretation is always informed by his clear vision of God's dealings with the whole of humanity, and human beings' dealings with one another, a vision that itself was formed by his reading of the Bible. Money, a severely practical matter, he regards as central to the teaching of the Bible and of Jesus; on the other hand he eschews anything that seems to him obscure or to have no bearing on practical Christian living in this world, for example the eschatological discourse in Mark, or which seems to him to be exclusive and to mark certain people out for special behaviour and special treatment, for example the farewell discourses in John – '[this] seems to me the most useless nonsense I ever read'.[11]

For Ruskin, the opposite of faith is not works but fear, 'the true use of faith is not to do away with deeds, but with fear'. He writes this in response to the story of Jesus stilling the storm, repeating and developing the idea in his discussion of the meaning of faith in the early chapters of Paul's letter to the Romans.[12] He believes this to be the message of the Bible, and he preaches it himself fearlessly. Underlying this attitude, in which Ruskin holds a thoroughly biblical vision of what it means to be human, is a strong and deeply personal belief in Providence and the Fatherly care of God for his children. Perfect love casts out fear. He repeatedly uses that beautiful image of children playing in the Father's garden, as birds do, learning above all things to get on well with each other in obedience to the good Father's ways.[13] With Karl Barth he might have said that Christian ethics was about 'the quiet and gentle and intimate awakening of children in the Father's house to life in that house'.[14]

In short Ruskin's approach to the Bible displays throughout his adult life a commitment to questioning and a commitment to the practical. His hermeneutical practice may be summed up as follows:

---

[9]   Burd, *Winnington Letters*, pp. 133–5.
[10] Egerton 3046, 136.3.2 (136V).
[11] Egerton 3046, 47R.
[12] Diaries 1858/1859, folio 125; Romans is discussed in folios 284–301.
[13] See also *Works*, 27, 206–7, 132–5, and Diaries 1858/1859, folio 171.
[14] Karl Barth, *Church Dogmatics IV, The Doctrine of Reconciliation*, trans. G.W. Bromiley (Edinburgh: T&T Clark, 1956), p. 100.

- an interrogative approach
- an ability to live with doubt and uncertainty
- an interest in his own personal reading history
- a partiality for justice and servanthood as the heart of the gospel
- a settled preference for practical obedience as the form of faith
- a dislike of religious exclusivity and arrogance
- a suspicion of the obscure, otherworldly, eschatological and 'mystic'.[15]

This list omits one key category, explored below, which is intimately linked to changes and developments in his life as he moved from a focus on art criticism to a focus on social criticism, and from a strict evangelicalism to a broader cultural approach.

Change and Growth in Understanding

In the years prior to 1858 Ruskin experienced a long process of religious questioning, during which he found himself unable to accept for himself and interiorise the evangelical faith of his upbringing. He gives three different accounts of the culminating experience in Turin in the summer of 1858, of which the following is found in his autobiography, *Praeterita*.

> The assembled congregation numbered in all some three or four and twenty, of whom fifteen or sixteen were grey-haired women. Their solitary and clerkless preacher, a somewhat stunted figure in a plain black coat, with a cracked voice, after leading them through the languid forms of prayer which are all that in truth are possible to people whose present life is dull and its terrestrial future unchangeable, put his utmost zeal into a consolatory discourse on the wickedness of the wide world, more especially of the plain of Piedmont and city of Turin, and on the exclusive favour with God, enjoyed by the between nineteen and twenty-four elect members of his congregation, in the streets of Admah and Zeboim.
>
> Myself neither cheered nor greatly alarmed by this doctrine, I walked back into the condemned city, and up into the gallery where Paul Veronese's Solomon and the Queen of Sheba glowed in the full afternoon light. The gallery windows being open, there came in with the warm air, floating swells and falls of military music, from the courtyard before the palace, which seemed to me more devotional, in their perfect art, tune, and discipline, than anything I remembered of evangelical hymns. And as the perfect colour and sound gradually asserted

[15] For further development of these categories in Ruskin's work, see Bennett, 'Ruskin, the Bible and the Death of Rose La Touche', and Zoë Bennett, '"A fact full of power or a dream full of meaning": The Influence of Religion and the Bible on Ruskin's Social, Political and Economic Critique', *Ruskin Review and Bulletin*, 6.2 (Autumn 2010): 35–47.

their power on me, they seemed finally to fasten me in the old article of Jewish faith,that things done delightfully and rightly, were always done by the help and in the Spirit of God.[16]

Normally, and rightly, related to the development of his understanding of beauty in relation to religion, this period in his life was, however, pivotal in another respect too. In 1860 he published the final volume of *Modern Painters* and also the first and most famous of his broadsides on political economy, *Unto This Last*. It may not be coincidence that the explicit moving away from evangelical religion and the moving towards a focused commitment to social justice came to a climax during the same period of time. They are marked, and linked together, among other things by an extraordinary series of notes in Ruskin's personal diaries of 1858 and 1859. The material is headed 'The Content of Faith' and is not included in the published version of the diaries.[17] It is interspersed among accounts of his travels in Europe with his parents, and all the drawings and weather observations, information about his health and personal feelings, and other materials that are the staples of Ruskin's diaries.

The section of this material of most interest here is a minutely detailed exegesis of the Greek text of the early chapters of Romans – the very material Ruskin knew contained the heart of evangelical faith. Of key concern to him is to understand two things: the meaning of *dikaiosune*, justice/righteousness, and the connection between faith and works. He seeks to understand 'the obedience of faith' (1.5). 'Justice' he interprets in the sense of right action, and with a focus on just treatment of others in the human community; 'Injustice', he writes, is here declared to be 'the great comprehensive Crime of crimes'.[18]

This deep work of personal wrestling with the text allowed Ruskin to carry forward into the second half of his life a sense that whatever changes the development of his faith brought he was not estranged from what he saw as the heart of Christianity, the love of God manifested in the life and works of Jesus Christ, and the call to live and work under God for human flourishing. It was a climate where many felt that they had lost their faith and were left with vestigial traces – in the poignant words of his French Catholic contemporary Ernest Renan: 'I sense that my life is always governed by a faith that I no longer have ... After Orpheus lost his perfect prize and was torn to shreds by the maenads, his lyre

[16]   *Works*, 35, 495–6.

[17]   Joan *Evans* and John Howard *Whitehouse (eds), The Diaries of John Ruskin*, 3 vols (Oxford: Clarendon, 1956–59).

[18]   Diaries 1858/1859, folio 287. Note also in *Unto this Last* that in 'Qui Judicatis Terram' Malachi 4.2 is translated as Sun of Justice; Ruskin argues in a footnote that 'righteousness' is too weak a word in common parlance to carry the meaning clearly (*Works*, 17, 59).

could sing no song but "Eurydice, Eurydice!"[19] Ruskin, however, believed that many Victorian Christians, even and especially the leaders of the churches, were the ones estranged from the true meaning of faith. Ruskin's faith was not torn to shreds, in spite of his own self-description as 'unconverted'. The evidence of his diary entries shows a man of intellectual and spiritual courage fighting to understand the nature of his faith better; and the evidence of his future writings demonstrates the integral nature of that biblical faith to the work he accomplished.

This period of strenuous examination of the biblical foundation of his faith is marked for Ruskin not only by new horizons in 'the content of faith', but also by a subtle but hugely significant change in the hermeneutical strategy he employed to understand the relationship between his biblical faith and the world around him. In a nutshell he moved from the classic, intra-biblical kind of typology, widespread among Victorians and particularly Victorian evangelicals, to a hermeneutic of immediacy and analogy which loosened the typological framework and widened it to include and indeed put at its heart the contemporary experience of the reader.

As a boy and young man Ruskin was deeply influenced by the typological methods of interpreting the Bible common in evangelical circles. He would have heard such interpretation in Sunday sermons, and he reproduced it in his own boyish attempts:

> I wish to follow up the shadow of sacrifice to its substance, Christ.// For, the law was raised up, in order/ to throw forward a shadow to another economy. (sic) which other economy, was,/ we see shadowed forth by sacrifice. & / this is explained in the beginning of the / 10th chapter, of Hebrews where it is said / that the law, having a shadow of good / things to come, and not the very image / of those things, can never with sacrifices, make the comers[?] thereunto perfect, & / it goes on to say that the blood of / bulls and goats can never take away / sin.[20]

Here in Ruskin's teenage 'sermons' both the law and the sacrifices of the Old Testament are seen as types or prefigurings of the antitype, the work of Christ. Such typological understanding in its widest sense, the seeing of the antitype type reflected and foreshadowed in the type and as a fulfilment of that type, influenced the Victorian mindset well beyond the strict sphere of religion. It could be used to relate not only events in the New Testament to events in the Old, but contemporary phenomena to biblical events, and spilled over into a secular form, as a way of construing a range of contemporary realities, including the political.[21]

---

[19] Ernest Renan, *Souvenirs d'Enfance et de Jeunesse* (Paris: Editions Gallimard, 1983), pp. 18–19 (my translation).

[20] Taken from a transcription of Ruskin's Sermon Notes on the Pentateuch (from the third volume of a set of five booklets) written when he was 12 or 13 years old. The transcription was prepared by Margaret Clunan, Documentation Assistant at the Ruskin Museum, Coniston, where the volume is held.

[21] Landow, *Victorian Types*.

Robert Hewison expounds Ruskin's aesthetic in his early writings in terms of the capacity of nature to be a 'type' of God's goodness and beauty to us, and then of art to represent that: 'Ruskin's theological view of the world asserts itself; types express the nature of God, through the material facts of the world in forms accessible to man.'[22] Just as he saw the type and foreshadowing of Christ's sacrifice, the greater reality, in the animal sacrifices of the Old Testament, so Ruskin saw nature as a 'shadow' of God the creator, and great art such as Turner's as a shadow of nature. They were to him almost sacramental – carrying a foretaste of the realities they typified:

> What revelations have been made to humanity inspired, or caught up to heaven, of things to the heavenly region belonging, have been either by unspeakable words, or else by their very nature incommunicable, except in types and shadows.[23]

I believe that as Ruskin moved away from a strictly evangelical understanding he moved beyond this typological understanding; building on it, however, rather than totally rejecting it. As a young man there is evidence that he had used a famous evangelical commentary by the Calvinist Thomas Scott,[24] but in later life he never normally deigned to use such things – Collingwood reports, 'Once in his rooms in Oxford I remember getting into a difficulty about the correct quotation of some passage. "Haven't you a concordance?" I asked. "I'm ashamed to say I have," he said.'[25] He was idiosyncratic in his interpretation, with his deep and lifelong immersion in the text, his working knowledge of Greek – he often used a Greek New Testament or a Septuagint (translation into Greek) Old Testament – and his self-confident, imaginative and analytic intelligence. His way of relating contemporary events to the biblical text moved into what I have termed a 'hermeneutic of immediacy', in which by an almost metaphorical move biblical material is overlaid onto contemporary experience or contemporary experience seen through the lens of biblical phrases and biblically informed commitments.[26]

This hermeneutic of immediacy, or hermeneutic of analogy, underlies his social critique in the same way the typological understanding underlies his aesthetic: new wineskins for new wine. It allows him to breathe; and crucially it allows him to insert contemporary human experience into the heart of his hermeneutic in a way that is determinative of his appropriation of the biblical text.[27] Experience drives his biblical interests and his interpretative choices.

---

[22]   Hewison, *Argument*, p. 58.

[23]   *Works*, 4, 208.

[24]   Michael Wheeler, *Ruskin's God* (Cambridge: Cambridge University Press, 1999), p. 18.

[25]   Collingwood, *Relics*, p. 211.

[26]   Bennett, 'Ruskin, the Bible and the Death of Rose La Touche'.

[27]   See Frei, *Eclipse*, for how this fits with contemporary moves in biblical hermeneutics.

It is not that this new hermeneutic is totally alien to the typological method. In a sense it grows out of it – just as it grows out of Ruskin's own previous journey. Taking another section of his boyhood sermons, 'the peace / offering ... which denotes, first/ly, the general peace and fellowship be/tween the offerers and God, the peace in / his own mind, and the peace between / him and the rest of mankind', we see how, unlike the more abstracted or theoretical tone of the first quotation from the sermons above, human experience is very close. What Ruskin does is develop from this his own way of connecting the two texts: life and the Bible.[28]

The Hermeneutic of Immediacy (Analogy)

This hermeneutical strategy is clear in Ruskin's daily readings in the Lectionary of 1875. Commenting, for example, on Matthew 27 where the chief priests will not put into the treasury the 30 pieces of silver Judas returns to them, because they are blood money, he writes: 'Our priests don't even warn our Chancellor of the Exchequer of such unlawfulness.'[29] Here Ruskin takes the biblical story and the contemporary story and overlays them so they each bring out more meaning from the other. The immorality of the capitalist economy is the main target of Ruskin's biblical opprobrium, but the church is not spared either.

A *Fors Clavigera* letter written in the same year displays Ruskin's general contempt for the bishops of the Church of England and particular distain for the then Bishop of Peterborough:

> Did he ever see a wolf coming and debate with himself whether he should fight or fly? – or is not rather his whole life one headlong hirelings flight without so much as turning his head to see what manner of beasts they are that follow? ... How many wolves does he know in Peterborough – how many sheep? ... what bite marks can he show the scars of?[30]

Here the same mode is used, an overlaying of the biblical story onto the contemporary scene, to bring out features of this contemporary scene and evaluate them, and to illuminate the meaning in practice of the biblical text. The strategy is striking, economical and involves the reading of 'multiple texts' – the biblical 'text' and the 'text' of contemporary life; it is predicated on clear seeing and yields plain telling.

Unto this Last contains a memorable ironic extended use of this mode of interpretation. He begins Essay 3, 'Qui Judicatis Terram', 'Some centuries before the Christian era, a Jew merchant, largely engaged in business on the Gold Coast

---

[28]   The typological method had been used by others such as Carlyle in analysing secular political history.

[29]   Egerton 3046, 65R.

[30]   *Works*, 28, 242–3. Reference to John 10.12.

... left among his ledgers some maxims concerning wealth.' Using the proverbs of Solomon the essay proceeds to develop a discussion of the relationship between wealth and human flourishing, ironically implying that the modern practical businessman has no use in his political economy for such wisdom:

> Nevertheless I shall reproduce a passage or two from them here ... chiefly because they will show [the reader] that it is possible for a very practical and acquisitive tradesman to hold, through a not unsuccessful career, that principle of distinction between well-gotten and ill-gotten wealth, which, partially insisted on in my last paper, it must be our work more completely to examine in this.[31]

While here there is a narrative and an exposition of maxims to accompany the hermeneutic of immediacy, the same basic strategy can be seen – the overlaying of the biblical picture of Solomon onto the current scene, the Jew merchant laid immediately against the contemporary merchant to stimulate comparison and to provoke the imaginative and moral faculties of the reader.

This can best be illustrated by a picture. Stanley Spencer (1891–1959) is famous for his paintings in which he overlays on each other a biblical story and a contemporary scene, often a scene from his home village of Cookham in Sussex. Take, for example, *Christ's Entry into Jerusalem* (c. 1920). In this picture we see Christ entering Cookham High Street as the biblical story is pictorially intertwined with a contemporary scene.[32] Our imaginations are invited to consider both Christ's entry into Jerusalem and Cookham of 1920 in a new light. As we look at the people in the picture, at their hurrying and scurrying, or at their going about their business in the usual way, at the four unmoved and unmoving figures on the right, we not only read the biblical story and a contemporary town, but are drawn in to place ourselves in the picture. We enter the hermeneutical circle of biblical world, reader's world and reader as we look.

It is in this kind of way that Ruskin lays the text of the contemporary world and the text of the biblical world on top of each other in our imagination, just as he literally lays his own written text on top of the biblical page in his annotations. This vivid and immediate way of connecting biblical text and world spills out from Ruskin's private Bible study and becomes a central feature of his extensive and continuous use of the Bible in his public speaking and writing. There are two important features to note in this way of working. First, it works by comparison and analogy, and second it works at the level of imaginative engagement.

It is in a sense a metaphorical way of working; in a metaphor two objects are verbally laid side by side so that by looking at them together our imaginations are provoked and we 'see' something new and fresh –

---

[31]   *Works*, 17, 57.
[32]   Available to view at http://www.bridgemanart.com/ (accessed 09.08.2012).

'this is like that'; 'this reminds me of that'; 'when I hear or see *this* I hear or see something new about both *this* and *that*'. The imagination is sparked by seeing or hearing in such a way that new associations are made, new insights achieved, new pain or new joy felt. Like the parables of Jesus, such bursts of imagination can create a fresh horizon of insight, and reflection on those insights develops understanding.[33]

Just as in Spencer's picture Jerusalem and Cookham are superimposed visually, so in Ruskin's laying together of Judas's return of the 30 pieces of silver to the chief priests and contemporary economic policy we are invited to question values, to consider the role of money and to open up questions of justice. 'What bite marks can he show the scars of?' entangles the modern Bishop and the good shepherd in our imagination so we are provoked to 'see' the self-indulgence and lack of care about which Ruskin is protesting. Ruskin's readers are challenged to see Solomon in his counting house, and plying his trade in ships on the high seas, and *at the same time* to see their own commercial and imperial world. This is a laying alongside – *analogy*; it is direct and without mediation – *immediate*.

In so doing Ruskin is not proof-texting, he is not primarily using texts to prove a particular prescriptive point or to trump other texts; he is working by resonance and analogy to open up our imagination and provoke our involvement. He does indeed make this more directly prescriptive kind of move in other places. For example, in his lecture in 1858 in Tunbridge Wells on the uses of iron, he brings out a string of references from the Psalms with which he berates his audience – such things were written for them, and they need to identify themselves as oppressors of the poor.[34] However, he is also capable of a much more complex appeal via the scriptures, and this capacity grows in him.

> Ye sheep without shepherd, it is not the pasture that has been shut from you, but the Presence. Meat! Perhaps your right to that may be pleadable; but other rights have to be pleaded first. Claim your crumbs from the table if you will; but claim them as children not as dogs; claim your right to be fed, but claim more loudly your right to be holy, perfect, and pure![35]

Here the references to the Bible are multiple, they are oblique and they are interspersed with one another and the readers' situation to catch the analogical imagination and resonate there. Ruskin evokes all the passages in the Bible about sheep and shepherds from Isaiah and Ezekiel to John 11 and 1 Peter, the Shekinah

---

[33]   Introduction to Bennett and Gowler (eds), *Radical Christian Voices*, p. 5. See Donald Davidson's exposition of what a metaphor is, or rather does, in Donald Davidson, 'What Metaphors Mean', in *Inquiries into Truth and Interpretation* (Oxford: Oxford University Press, 1984), pp. 245–64.

[34]   See Chapter 8, p. 101.

[35]   *Works*, 17, 107.

and the Holy of Holies, the feeding of the children of Israel in the desert, the gospel story of the Syrophoenician woman, Dives and Lazarus, and the many references to holiness, perfection and purity.

'Resonance and analogy' is one of the categories used by Roger Walton in his typology of ways in which we read the Bible and relate it to our lives.[36] His schema runs from proof-texting and links and associations on the one hand to the intellectual rigours of mutual critique and correlation on the other, with resonance and analogy somewhere in the middle. The great merits of the resonance and analogy model are its invitation to the imagination and its dependence on the experience of the reader as the imaginative (analogous and resonant) correlate of the scriptures. Just as analogy sets things side by side so we may see them together, so 'resonance' does the same for hearing. Resonance is 'sound produced by a body vibrating in sympathy with a neighbouring source of sound' (Collins English Dictionary). This opens up the idea that an interpreter, or a community of interpreters, find themselves moved ('vibrating') as what they read in the Bible sets off in them emotions, actions, thoughts and perspectives which have connections with what is read sufficient to respond, but which are expanded and activated by that reading. In turn the scriptures themselves 'vibrate' with freshly understood meaning. The imagination is expanded, allowed to 'play' and, crucially for Ruskin, challenged by the scriptures, in ways that mesh with contemporary life, action and culture.[37]

This way of engaging the Bible with contemporary life has been criticised for its alleged 'collapsing [of the] eschatological tension' between 'now' and the 'not yet' world of Christian hope: it 'sell[s] God's "permanent revolution" short. The theological imagination must not be prematurely brought to equilibrium with the reality that is already given.'[38] But equilibrium is the last thing in Ruskin's mind. These analogies serve to turn the world of their hearers and readers upside-down. They operate as Moltmann said of eschatological hope, 'as a thorn in the side of the present' to goad us into action in the face of injustice.[39]

Such a hermeneutical approach – the superimposition of the biblical text on the contemporary reality to bring each to life – has links with interpretative strategies of both past and present. It is embedded in the heart of our biblical text as one of the methods used by Paul to link the Jewish scriptures with the contemporary context of the early Christians, as we saw in Chapter 1:

---

[36]   Roger Walton, 'Using the Bible and Christian Tradition in Theological Reflection', *British Journal of Theological Education*, 13.2 (January 2003): 133–51.

[37]   Rowland and Bennett, 'New Testament Theology and Practical Theology'.

[38]   Jeremy Law, 'Theological Imagination and Human Flourishing', in Mike Higton, Jeremy Law and Christopher Rowland (eds), *Theology and Human Flourishing: Essays in Honor of Timothy J. Gorringe* (Eugene, Ore.: Wipf and Stock, 2011), p. 297.

[39]   Jürgen Moltmann, *Theology of Hope: On the Ground and the Implications for a Christian Eschatology* (London: SCM Press, 2002; first published in German, 1965), p. 21.

> I do not want you to be unaware, brothers and sisters, that our ancestors were all
> under the cloud, and all passed through the sea, and all were baptized into Moses
> in the cloud and in the sea, and all ate the same spiritual food, and all drank the
> same spiritual drink. For they drank from the spiritual rock that followed them,
> and the rock was Christ. (1 Cor. 10.1–4)

Here Paul admonishes his contemporaries in Corinth on the basis of their self-
understanding engendered and imaginatively engaged by this recalling of the story
of their spiritual ancestors' wanderings and rebellion. The passage is functioning
in the same way as Ruskin's evocations of the biblical text.

The approach surfaces in the concerns of an ancient interpreter, Tyconius.
Tyconius (c. 330–90) was an older contemporary of Augustine, who had a profound
effect on him. His method of interpretation presumed the unity of the Bible and the
world.[40] In his exegetical rules he insisted that the Bible spoke of the Church as
Christ's body well as of Christ himself, and thus as Christ is linked to the Church
as head to body there is always possible overlap in the applicability of texts. This
makes possible contemporary, ecclesial, interpretation of the Bible. Ruskin stands
in this tradition of intimate linkage between biblical world and present reality.

In the twentieth century the method of biblical exegesis offered by liberation
theology affords another example of relating texts to life. This is classically
laid out by Clodovis Boff as a model of 'correspondence of terms'. In this two
'realities' – the biblical and the contemporary – are directly compared. Boff finds
this to be hermeneutically inadequate and offers instead his 'correspondence of
relationships' which requires an analysis of relationships going on in the biblical
text and likewise in the contemporary world, and then a comparison of the
relationships, the products of this analysis.[41] This is a move to incorporate the
socio-analytical into the heart of biblical interpretation – both on the biblical text
'horizon' and on the contemporary horizon. Ruskin's method is more immediate,
working with the imagination and with 'the hermeneutic of immediacy' rather
than with sociological analysis, though deeply fired by social concerns and his
own response to social ills. It is more akin, therefore, to Boff's 'correspondence
of terms' model.

Summing Up and Moving On

This book has been substantially concerned first with ourselves as readers of the
Bible, and then with John Ruskin, a reader who may be a mirror to us, as we
negotiate, sometimes painfully, our relationship to that Bible in the context of
our relationships with others and our growing understanding of God. Just as we

---

[40] Maureen A. Tilley, *The Bible in Christian North Africa: The Donatist World*
(Minneapolis, Minn.: Augsburg Fortress, 1997), p. 116.

[41] Boff, *Theology and Praxis*.

are already 'thrown' into the story that is our contemporary world, so we already indwell the text of the Bible, and it indwells us. We are not coming from nowhere, but from a history in which we are shaped by the Christian tradition, and its primary text, and within which we have our own ongoing history of wrestling with it. Our own 'reading history' determines our engagement with the Bible, and our engagement of the Bible in public issues. It does not fix us in such a way that we are deterministically stuck in one place for ever, but shapes the ongoing story of our struggle to relate the Bible and contemporary life. In this our feelings about the Bible matter as much as our intellectual grasp; our practices of reading it count for as much as our struggles with the ways we have been taught it.

A further crucial matter of concern has been how the text of the Bible and the text of life might be related. Ruskin has opened up for us a possibility of relating ancient text and current context. We have seen an example of *how* the Bible might be related to contemporary life. There are two features of this that we observed in Ruskin. The first is foundational, and is a matter of how he himself relates the Bible to life. The second is what we might term strategic – not so much foundational to his own thinking but rather a way of using the Bible publicly that will make sense to his readers. Both features are necessary to consider, in our own case as well as in Ruskin's – the foundational and the strategic.

The foundational aspect to how Ruskin relates the Bible and contemporary life is about *comparison* and about *imaginative engagement*. Working analogically it sets side by side the chief priests receiving Judas's money and the Chancellor of the Exchequer, Solomon and contemporary merchant classes, the iron railings of industrial foundries and the injunctions of the Psalms. Ruskin is constantly reading the story of his own time through the story of the Bible and vice versa, for mutual illumination. It is important to notice that although within this there is much passion and conviction it is fundamentally not a method of using the Bible prescriptively, but persuasively. Ruskin writes: 'It is not, therefore, because I am endeavouring to lay down a foundation of religious concrete, on which to build piers of policy, that you so often find me quoting Bible texts in defence of this or that principle or assertion.'[42] He uses this method to persuade, in order that we might be engaged and provoked to respond by a gestalt move, an aha moment in which our fundamental source of conviction and value is laid alongside the realities of our contemporary lives in stark juxtaposition.

The strategic aspect of this is that Ruskin is always conscious of his readers' attitudes to the Bible. He does not blunder on, using a text in ways that mean nothing to those who hear. While his own deepest convictions are biblically informed and related, he carefully crafts how he uses this to persuade in the public realm, engaging the convictions of his hearers. The entirety of letter VIII of *Time and Tide* is devoted to examining the views of his contemporaries on the Bible, in minute detail, and to explaining how his use of the Bible in his political writings is deliberately designed to catch the sentiments and convictions of the highest

---

[42]   *Works*, 17, 348.

number of people.[43] This aspect of public use of the Bible will become more centrally our theme in Part III.

But first we look at what is perhaps the most significant contribution John Ruskin makes to the use of the Bible in public theology – his emphasis on the centrality of sight. The art of seeing clearly is essential. Whether we are looking at the Bible or at a painting, at God's clouds and water or at the human artefacts that tell the story of our social injustices, there is no substitute for careful, attentive seeing. Good sight is the foundation for all truth telling, for all imaginative empathy and for all inspiration. The next three chapters will explore how Ruskin invites us and inspires us to see better.

In writing this I am acutely aware that there are practical theologians who are not able to see physically. While much of what Ruskin has to say when he is talking about art is in relation to actual physical sight, the application to practical theology is by analogy. The significant facility is the facility accurately and attentively to register and receive that which presents itself to us, whatever senses and whatever means we use to do that.

---

[43]   'Things Written: The Four possible Theories respecting the Authority of the Bible', March 7th 1867, *Works*, 17, 348–51.

Chapter 6
On Seeing Clearly

To be taught to read – what is the use of that, if you know not whether what you read
is false or true? To be taught to write or to speak – but what is the use of speaking,
if you have nothing to say? To be taught to think – nay, what is the use of being able
to think, if you have nothing to think of? But to be taught to see is to gain word and
thought at once, and both true.[1]

The quotation that heads this chapter and many scattered throughout it are taken
from Ruskin's inaugural lecture for the founding of the Cambridge School of
Art in 1858; drawing was to Ruskin the supreme practice in which a person
could learn to see well. At the root of all good practical and public theology
is good seeing. Attention to the specifics in front of us constitute the basic
first move in a whole range of theological methods associated with practical,
pastoral, political, liberation or contextual theology. This may be expressed as a
requirement for 'attention', drawing on Simone Weil's suggestive work.[2] It may
be expressed as a direct injunction to see – as in the 'see, judge, act' method
used widely and explicitly from the 1960s, originating in Catholic social
teaching and methods and associated with the name of Cardinal Joseph Cardijn,
founder of the Young Christian Workers movement. It may be implied by the
very method of setting up reflection, as in the *verbatim* method used in Clinical
Pastoral Education where a student prepares a word for word account of a
pastoral encounter and presents this to a group for analysis. All such methods
require first the art of observation.

It is critical to know what constitutes *good* 'seeing'. As John Ruskin says, upon
good seeing depends our capacity to make judgments, to communicate anything
worthwhile or to have any material fit for reflection. Seeing does not only furnish
us with imagination; good seeing makes possible evaluation and discernment. In
other words, it makes possible not only knowledge, but also wisdom.

But what is required for good seeing? In this chapter and the next two we will
take Ruskin as our guide. There is much to learn from him, as he was one of the
great masters of seeing well, and, fortunately for us, he not only did it but talked,
wrote and theorised about it. There are three great truths about seeing well that

---

[1]   Ruskin, *Works*, 16, 180.

[2]   Jane Leach, 'Pastoral Theology as Attention', *Contact. Practical Theology and
Pastoral Care*, 153 (2007): 19–32; Janet Martin Soskice, 'Love and Attention', in *The
Kindness of God* (Oxford: Oxford University Press, 2007), pp. 7–34.

stand out in Ruskin's practice and theory: clear sight, heart sight and prophetic sight. These three give our chapters' content.

We begin with *seeing clearly*, and note three features of clear sightedness: seeing with faithful precision, the capacity to describe and lingering with, or taking time with, the object of our observation.

Faithful Precision

I once received a letter from my mother, an excellent letter-writer, then on holiday in Scotland, in which she stated: 'There was a man behind us in Birnie's this morning in a raincoat, eating a bun and a banana, and buying a newspaper.' It has always struck me how much more she told me by these precise details than by some general statements of activity accompanied by conventional adjectives. Of course description is always already selective and freighted with meaning and interpretation; nevertheless, most methods of reflection in pastoral and practical theology begin with an invitation to report a scenario, in spoken or written form, telling precisely what happened – what did people say, what were their body movements, what did they wear, eat, buy, read and so on? Likewise public theology begins in factual information – who is involved, for how long has this been happening, where does the money come from, how many people do this, what age are they, what institutions are involved, what political parties support this, how? Before analysis, sociological or theological, before considered interpretation and judgment, before commitment and action, as much information as possible, observed and reported as accurately and as clearly and plainly as possible, needs to be accessed. 'I've made up my mind; don't confuse me with facts', is not an attitude conducive to understanding truth or to making good judgments.

Ruskin gave drawing lessons throughout much of his life and valued highly the skill of observing and copying. He studied and drew in exact detail birds, feathers, flowers, water, rocks and buildings, and other people's paintings. This he encouraged his pupils also to do, in order to sharpen their powers of observation. In later life, as Slade Professor of Art at Oxford University, Ruskin used his own drawings to illustrate his lectures, dividing them into four series, making catalogues and designing frames to display and cabinets to store them.[3] Ruskin had the eye of a bird, a sketcher's eye, noting every vein of a leaf, every shadow in a rock, 'every subtle gradation of tender light and flickering form', less interested in mass and structure than in itemising the 'minute particulars' which render reality to us.[4]

---

[3]   See Nicholas Penny, *Ruskin's Drawings* (Oxford: Ashmolean Museum, 2004) and the wonderful collection online at http://ruskin.ashmolean.org/ (accessed 26.01.2012).

[4]   See John Drury, 'Ruskin's Way: tout a fait comme un oiseau', in S. Collini, R. Whitmore and B. Young (eds), *History, Religion, and Culture: British Intellectual History, 1750–1950* (Cambridge: Cambridge University Press, 2000), pp. 156–76, at pp. 162–3. For

Drawing for Ruskin was always a way to see better, not an end in itself. In *The Elements of Drawing*, published in 1857, he wrote,

> For I am early convinced that, when once we see keenly enough, there is very little difficulty in drawing what we see; but, even supposing that this difficulty be still great, I believe that the sight is a more important thing than the drawing; and I would rather teach drawing that my pupils would learn to love Nature, than teach the looking at Nature that they may learn to draw.[5]

Notwithstanding this primary orientation to the object rather than the drawing of it, the facility of good seeing is enhanced for Ruskin, even engendered, by practice in good drawing, for the technical skill of drawing is a way into the deeper skill of sight. Sight itself is the most important thing; even light, so beloved of religious discourse, is of little value without sight: 'It doesn't matter how much light you have, if you don't know how to use it.'[6]

Description

If the ultimate purpose of drawing is to enhance the facility for sight, it also has some secondary purposes:

> that you may be able to set down clearly, and usefully, records of such things as cannot be described in words, either to assist your own memory of them, or to convey distinct ideas of them to other people; [if you wish] to obtain quicker perceptions of the natural world, and to preserve something like a true image of beautiful things that pass away or which you must leave.[7]

Ruskin's statement that some things cannot be described in words is suggestive for the possibility that public theological reflection might be rendered in some other form than the verbal. It is also somewhat ironical, coming from the man whose capacity to describe the paintings of others in English prose is second to none.[8]

---

the reference to 'minute particulars', see Blake's *Jerusalem*: 'He who would do good to another must do it in Minute Particulars. General Good is the plea of the scoundrel hypocrite & flatterer: For Art and Science cannot exist but in minutely organized Particulars And not in generalizing Demonstrations of the Rational power', Blake, p. 687.

[5] *Works*, 15, 13.
[6] *Works*, 16, 180.
[7] *Works*, 15, 25.
[8] A further issue concerning description is that the medium in which something is described changes how the viewer/listener perceives it. This is a technique known as *ekphrasis*, the retelling of something in a new medium. When Ruskin gives a verbal description of Turner's *Snow Storm – Steam Boat off a Harbour's Mouth* the verbal text renders the picture to us, and at the same time presents its material to the reader in quite

However that may be, he lays out here four reasons why we might wish to describe and to portray, whether it be in drawing, words or music, that which we see. These are, first, so that we ourselves remember them accurately; second, that we enable other people to see and understand them better; third, because the act of recording and rendering enhances our capacity to appreciate what we see; and finally, so that what is transient may not be lost entirely. An excellent example of the last point is his own meticulous drawing of the buildings of Venice, threatened on the one hand by destruction and on the other by crass preservation techniques.

All of these are excellent reasons why in various ways in pastoral, practical and public theology we might want to make accurate descriptions and portrayals of what we see. Indeed we record not only what we see but what we hear, smell, taste and touch/feel. Crucially there is a place also for the recording of our own emotional reactions, what we 'feel' in a different sense of the word, and this point opens up a problematic in any account of 'description' that leaves out the act of interpretation. All description is already interpretation, involving selection, highlighting and construction.

The aspiring doctor learns how to 'clerk', how to record symptoms and observations minutely. This is a prerequisite for understanding but this in itself is not understanding. However, even in the act of 'clerking' – in recording for our remembrance, in re-presenting to other people, in portraying in order to enhance appreciation and in preservation – we are at the very least making choices about what to convey and shaping this by the mode of conveyance. We are not fossilising something but making it live. Did Ruskin fossilise Venice? Yes and no. He attempted to record accurately what the buildings looked like, but he also wanted to do it in such a way as would engage the imagination of each succeeding generation, and for them to see its beauty for themselves. Ruskin wrestled with this problematic, the need on the one hand to represent details accurately, to 'clerk', and on the other to engage with the interpretation that might lead the original viewer and the reader of the account into deeper truth. He is consequently ambivalent about what might count as 'truth' – is it realistic rendering or imaginative penetration?

How does this question relate to the kind of seeing and describing that takes place in the context of theological reflection? An example of pastoral

---

a different way from the visual text to the viewer. For example, it starts somewhere and moves through features diachronically, whereas when we see the picture we see it in one go, synchronically, although of course our eye is drawn somewhere first, but is it the same place as Ruskin starts with? The comparison can easily be made by comparing Ruskin's description *Works*, 3, 569–71, available at http://www.lancs.ac.uk/fass/ruskin/empi/3rdedition/3b374.htm and the following two pages, with Turner's image http://www.tate.org.uk/art/artworks/turner-snow-storm-steam-boat-off-a-harbours-mouth-n00530. See Zoë Bennett, 'Creation Made Image and Image Made Word: John Ruskin on JMW Turner's "Snow Storm"', in D. Pezzoli-Olgiati and C. Rowland (eds), *Approaches to Visuality in Religion*, Research in Contemporary Religion (Göttingen: Vandenhoeck und Ruprecht, 2011), pp. 249–60.

description will illustrate the point here. A pastor presents a case study involving a conversation between youth leaders and a person who talks to them about self-harming – a pastoral case with clear implications for public issues. He chooses to name their ages and gender but not their ethnic origin or social class. When asked why, he is clear – age and gender matter for safeguarding reasons, to do with legal requirements. They are also to do with expectations within his Christian community of how males and females should relate pastorally. Ethnic origin and social class are out of sight, though many people would have included them since 'race' and class analysis is a common contemporary interest. In another cultural context physical appearance might have been described, or the person's parents presented, if these were matters of contextual cultural interest. What has been 'seen' is determined by pre-existing interests, and at the description stage that determination, that selection process, is taken even further and reinforced. So in laying out models of theological reflection, for a 'pastoral cycle' of analysis, we must be clear that step one, description, is already a budding interpretation.

Furthermore, there are some descriptions where even to state what can be claimed as a 'bald fact' is in itself, or can invite, interpretation, even subconscious interpretation. Consider the use of the term 'woman-driver' in describing an incident in an insurance claim. It is a loaded term, factually accurate though it may be. It conjures up images for the reader which may prejudice their understanding. The self-harmer was named as female. This in itself may have brought to mind for the readers a 'typical' picture of the 'needy and attention-seeking' female. This is a stereotype, but one easily invoked. On the other hand not to name her as female is to miss an important piece of information. 'Female' is in itself a description which not only names facts (biological gender) but also conveys a construction (social gender). So even the 'facts' already carry interpretations. There are no bare facts.

Lingering

> And to this painting – in which it took me six weeks to examine rightly two figures – I found that on average the English traveller who was doing Italy conscientiously and seeing Italy 'as he ought,' gave about half or three quarters of a minute; but the flying or fashionable traveler, who came to do as much as he could in a given time never gave more than a single glance.

Ruskin is referring to his recent stay in Turin to examine the painting of the presentation of the Queen of Sheba to Solomon by Paul Veronese. Enraptured by the gorgeousness of the picture he had a kind of stage erected by the door over which the painting was hung in order to see and copy it more closely: 'One day I was upwards of two hours vainly trying to render, with perfect accuracy, the curves of two leaves of the brocaded silk.' From here he had a bird's eye view of the visitors passing through, and of their attentiveness, or lack of it, to that which was filling his eyes, his imagination and his soul. [9]

Seeing clearly takes time. As I read Ruskin's description I flinch at how often I have done exactly this, hurrying by and glancing without really seeing – in art exhibitions, when being introduced to people, skim-reading, surfing the internet. Information overload is a problem many times more grave today than it was in Ruskin's day, and the art of searching for what we do want to focus on in the plethora of what is thrust at us or easily available is a crucial one. But Ruskin's reminder to look at one thing well rather than many things skimpily is timely: 'To study one good master till you understand him will teach you more than a superficial acquaintance with a thousand.' [10]

It is one thing to enjoin lingering; quite another to do it. Lingering is hard because it involves time (which we feel we are short of) and it involves standing back mentally from that high level of frenetic activism in which we are semi-permanently engaged. Stilling our minds is as difficult if not more difficult than stilling our bodies. Driven activity is a drug, and is much easier than stillness. In stillness we may genuinely look at what is before us, and we may begin to see what is inside us too.

I am involved in a women's peace group that holds regular vigils in Cambridge market place. We stand, dressed in black, for one hour, in silence. Never am I so acutely observant of what is before me – what people are wearing, what shapes and sizes they are, their ages and the looks on their faces. I am aware of myself standing in a public place looking odd, of the ancient buildings of Cambridge, of what people are selling on their stalls and sometimes of their hostility or welcome. The discipline of an hour's silence standing in line in that context is hard – it gets boring, frustrating (just think what you could be getting on with!), you cannot distract yourself by chatting, by getting a coffee, by wandering around. In this particular case, of course, the observing is a sideline to the main purpose of the vigil, but this regular discipline has taught me a great deal about the need to be still, with time, in order to see more clearly.

'Mostly, matters of any consequence are three-sided, or four-sided, or polygonal; and the trotting round a polygon is severe work for people any way stiff in their opinions.' [11] Trotting round a polygon, used here by Ruskin as a picture of changing his mind several times before he feels he has understood something, furnishes another image for that lingering, that taking time to see something clearly. Here the discipline and difficulties are not so much stilling oneself as making the old bones move – loosening up the limbs of one's opinions and fixed ways of seeing things. Furthermore, the object in front of me is not simple; it needs to be seen from several sides, several perspectives, which may require me to move and to

---

[9]   *Works*, 16, 186. Note that it was this painting that figured in Ruskin's account of his 'unconversion', see Chapter 5, pp. 69-70.

[10]   *Works*, 16, 182.

[11]   *Works*, 16, 187.

see afresh, or to turn it round and look at a different angle. What Ruskin alludes to here is another thing that takes time and lingering – the exploration of something from various points of view. This is also a discipline: not just the acceptance of the obvious or even the joy of discovery, but also the critical questions, the probing for what might deny or contradict what seems obvious.

Beyond the First Clear Seeing

There remain two important considerations of Ruskin's view of clear-sightedness. First, there is a connection between even this basic form of clear seeing and Ruskin's 'seeing' of the Bible. His eye of a bird picks out jewels from the text in front of him. He works with the matter of the text, not with architecturally built theological themes.[12] He attends to translations, to the physical gold lettering of the manuscript, to words, to injunctions, to pictures, to individual verses. He reads and he re-reads; he never tires of the material in front of his nose.

But his seeing goes beyond this, to prophetic seeing and the sight of the heart. Just as Ruskin knows that the Bible or any object of our sight is like a polygon, in that there are many ways of looking at it, many perspectives, so he also knows that the kind of seeing that can describe 'what is in front of our noses' with exactness of detail is just the beginning of good sight; there is much more to come by way of imaginative penetration. Clarity of observational sight for Ruskin was an indispensable first step, but it was incomplete without passion and moral vision and above all understanding. Thus his laying of the two realities side by side, in the analogical method described in the previous chapter, is not only a creatively imaginative, quasi-pictorial comparison, but is generated by passion and moral vision in Ruskin and depends for its power on the engagement of these qualities in his readers. In the next two chapters we turn to examine further these qualities of good seeing.

---

[12]   Drury, 'Ruskin's Way'.

Chapter 7
On Seeing with the Heart

On holiday in Brittany I sat one morning by a grave over 5,000 years old. At the mouth of the Jaudy Estuary the 'covered alley' of Men ar Rompet lies on the headland, huge lichen encrusted stones roofing the narrow chamber. How did they lift such stones? I wanted to photograph them but somehow that didn't capture enough. As I lingered I began to wonder – *why* did I want to record, to describe? Three of Ruskin's four reasons applied: so I could go on remembering them; to convey them to others; that by looking more attentively I might enter more deeply into their reality.[1] As I sat and looked I felt drawn to think of the lives and deaths of those who were buried there so long ago. They looked out on the beautiful headland, sea and estuary, as from their graves my mother and father look out over the hills of Galloway, and my son over the trees and park in Bedford and my brother over the wide Essex cornfields. I realised that in addition to lingering and looking with precision, to walking round and considering, to describing accurately, there is human sympathy – a sense of the 'tears of things', Virgil's 'lacrimae rerum', community of spirit with all things human. Ruskin had this supremely. To know him or any human being more intimately, he said, we must learn to read the 'torn manuscripts of the human soul'.[2] Although it is a prerequisite, seeing clearly is not enough; we need 'heart-sight' as well as eyesight.[3]

The Engagement of the Self

Heart-sight will require that we insert ourselves into the process. It was only by analogy with my own experience of burying my dead and visiting their graves that I was able even to begin to approach the experience of other human beings. Of course this is only an approach, an analogy; there are many differences between my experience and theirs. But it is an essential start.

The importance of attending to self-involvement is rightly stressed in both theological reflection and biblical hermeneutics. As interpreters both of written texts and of the 'living human document' it is vital to identify where we are coming

---

[1]   See Chapter 6, p. 84.
[2]   *Works*, 18, 28.
[3]   *Works*, 7, 377.

from and what presuppositions, cognitive and affective, we are bringing with us. This self-attentiveness serves to alert ourselves and our own readers to biases, blind spots and partial views. It also serves to bring what we see into sharper focus through good use of our lenses, as is made clear in Schleiermacher's humanistic and psychologically oriented approach to hermeneutics.[4]

This can work in one of two ways. The first is by analogy, as in the example above. This is a kind of 'laying alongside'. I lay alongside the grave at Men ar Rompet a grave in Kirkcudbright, looking out over the Galloway Hills. This is prompted initially by the similarity of natural beauty – the sea, the river, the heathland and perhaps the similarity of stone marking a human grave. Maybe it is also stimulated by the imagination – of men carrying a human body and laying it in the grave; and by the difference – what does it mean to lay a body under an alleyway of stones rather than in the ground? What did it mean to bury someone so long ago – did they die so much younger or without medicine and in pain? And I feel – I feel the loss, and the calming effect of the landscape, and the liminality, the sense of human beings on the edge of nature and on the edge of eternity, such a frail world, but our whole world. So now I lay alongside that grave not only my parents' grave but my own feelings as a human being. They are not the feelings of the women and men of 5000 BCE; I will never have anything like full access to what those are. But there is a deep-seated conviction about commonality of humanity, however culturally and socially conditioned each generation may be, and on that commonality rests the conviction that one may 'read' the texts of the human document, even of those who lived thousands of years ago. It rests on information gained from the traces they have left, the creation of the picture by historical research; but my heart-sight is an indispensable beginning to the process of accessing that picture.

This is so in all attempts to read the human document: the analogy, the likeness and the unlikeness. 'I know just what you are feeling' must always be wrong; yet 'I have been there' – or somewhere like it – is part of understanding: not the only part, and 'somewhere *like* it' is crucial. There is a thin but essential line of difference between claiming to know exactly and being able to enter imaginatively via analogous experience. In seeing this we begin to see why understanding that comes by self-involvement may be so potentially distorted; our own baggage, our own pain and joy, our own perspectives are the most difficult to see and understand well, and have a huge potential to block or to overwhelm, and thus to distort, our vision of that which is outside ourselves. But there is no alternative in interpretation but to take the risk of exploring imaginatively and 'with the heart'. Without it we would be left with the enigmas of the *vestigia*.

Besides the analogical there is a second way in which bringing ourselves and our feelings to our vision of the living human document and its 'texts' may enable understanding. To develop further what was mentioned in Chapter 2, in psychoanalysis there is a process known as 'counter-transference'. Part of this

---

[4]   See Chapter 3.

process is that the therapist feels something, some emotions perhaps, in themselves towards the patient/client. This can be problematic if undetected and unreflected upon, but it can, on the other hand, be a learning process, because through this the therapist learns something about what the person in analysis is 'projecting' onto them. Put simply, if the analyst feels hugely protective this may give a clue to a yearning for protection which the person in analysis is giving off.

Moving away from the Neolithic grave to another analogy: imagine instead watching an emotionally powerful film with a group of friends. As you begin to discuss afterwards everyone has a contribution: some can tell you where this film fits in the director's work, some about the historical context of its setting, others about what genre of film it is and what other films it quotes. Some discuss the ideas in the film; others the turns of the plot. One person is boringly predictable; she always tells the group how she feels. I have come to see that this is not a purely self-oriented outpouring; it is a possible clue to understanding the film, backwards from its effects.

Our own reactions, feelings and emotions, do not tell directly but indirectly about the object we are reacting to. They may also mislead us; because their origin is in ourselves as well as in the 'object' we are attempting to scrutinise and interpret. But they are not thereby irrelevant nor a hindrance to understanding; they are an indispensable part of understanding in practical theology. This is because the object we are interpreting is either a human being (a living human document) or some trace or text left behind by a human being, their vestigial tracks. This is true of a gravestone, or a film, or the text of the Bible. These are all created by human beings and deal with human issues, leave traces – intentional or unintentional – of the human being, and only make sense in terms of the human beings implicit in their existence. So just like the process of counter-transference in therapy, our reactions as human beings give us clues via our empathy to what is in those people and their traces, their '*vestigia*', and how we might understand them. This is part of Ruskin's heart-sight.

The possibility of being misled is ever-present in all interpretation. Here the very source of our understanding of others, our own reactions, may obscure rather than enlighten, if our own reactions are not properly reflected upon and analysed. Hence for the therapist it is vital that they are supervised in their work by someone who can help them to do this. Similarly in theological reflection, there need to be mechanisms in place to aid analysis and to illuminate and clarify the role of the self. There are many possibilities, ranging from supervised reflective practice groups to disciplined steps and models of theological reflection that ask probing questions. When we listen to ourselves, or others listen to us, carefully, critically and creatively, heart-sight flourishes.

The Engagement of the Emotions

It is in the final volume of *Modern Painters* that Ruskin introduces the concept of heart-sight. He compares two boyhoods – that of Giorgioni in the marbled purity of Venice with its clear Italian air, and that of Turner in the streets of Covent Garden strewn with cabbages and oranges, or by the Thames in the 'mist of early sunbeams', crowded with debris, boats and boatmen. Turner, he claimed, learned here 'sensibility to human distress and affection ... no less keen than even his sense for natural beauty – heart-sight deep as eyesight'.[5] By 'heart-sight' Ruskin means the engagement of the emotions and the will in an integrated ethical and aesthetic vision – vision in the sense of both clear seeing and of commitment.

Comparing Claude's picture of the building of Carthage with Turner's – which hang side by side in the National Gallery in London at Turner's request – Ruskin points out that Claude embellishes his picture with the conventional detail of a carried trunk; Turner paints in small children playing with a toy boat – unconventional, directing the imagination to the communal and playful realities of human life, and to the 'ruling passion [ships and the sea] which was to be the source of future greatness'.[6] The name Ruskin gave in his aesthetic theory to the capacity to do more than copy precisely was penetrative imagination. While there are technical aspects to what he understood by this, an essential component is heart-sight, which sees beneath the surface into the depths of human life.

'Fearlessly and pitifully' is how he described the way we must see, 'gazing without shrinking into the darkness'.[7] In using this expression he was referring to how the artist needs to observe dark as well as light in order to see and show colour properly. It was written at a time, however, when he was moving from an interest in landscape painting to an interest in human life, towards that 'turn to the human' in which he sees and portrays human misery.[8]

Courage and pity – virtues nourished by the emotions as well as the will – are complemented in good seeing by love and delight. Why is French couture so much better than English, French silk dresses so much more beautiful than English silk dresses, asks Ruskin? Because the Englishwoman's only interest in the silk dress is that in it she should outdo her neighbour, but the French love silk. They are captivated by its beauty, take 'delight in the beauty and play of the silken folds and colours themselves, for their own gorgeousness or grace'; so they see its possibilities.[9]

[5]   *Works*, 7.377.
[6]   *Works*, 3, 113.
[7]   *Works*, 7, 271.
[8]   Zoë Bennett, '"To see fearlessly, pitifully": What Does John Ruskin Have to Offer to Practical Theology?', *International Journal of Practical Theology*, 14.2 (2011): 189–203.
[9]   *Works*, 16, 184–5.

These diverse examples all point us in one direction; if we wish to see well we cannot avoid a holistic engagement of the self and the emotions.[10] We cannot detach our feelings, nor can we detach what might be called our virtues, our priorities, what we care most about and are intentionally engaged with. Such seeing penetrates beneath the surface with imagination, with courage and with love. In Ruskin there was an intimate connection between good seeing that looked at pictures, landscape and architecture, entering 'intelligently into their beauty and significance' and good seeing that 'understood so clearly and taught so fearlessly the laws of social justice and brotherly kindness'.[11] These words carry us into the fierce passion of prophetic seeing, which is the subject of the next chapter. They are Collingwood's words, written to explain to the world the symbolism he carved on the stone cross on Ruskin's grave in the churchyard at Coniston in 1900, where Ruskin lies, mostly unnoticed and undisturbed, under the trees and the wet grass of the Lake District.

A 'Humanistic' Tradition of Interpretation

Before moving on, however, to prophetic seeing, there are some issues arising from the chapter thus far that need to be explored further.

Ruskin brings to his biblical interpretation not only the tradition of typological understanding which he shared with many Victorians, but also that tradition running 'from German pietism through the work of Schleiermacher and Dilthey down to Gadamer', which saw the interpretation of written texts in itself as a kind of interpretation of living human documents, in which the human interpreter meets the human author and understands him, to which the human interpreter brings all his presuppositions, and in which the moment of application is an essential part of the moment of interpretation.[12] Such interpretation enriches life. In this view the interpretation of the Bible is seen as involving essentially the same kind of act of interpretation as the interpretation of all texts, and indeed can be seen to be in a continuous tradition with the later interpretation of 'the living human document' within practical theology.

Anton Boisen, in founding the Clinical Pastoral Education movement in the United States in the 1930s, spoke of the need for trainee pastors to study not only written texts in the classroom but the living human document in field placements. Having spent some time personally as a patient in a psychiatric hospital, and having a deep grasp of what he had learned through this experience, he was keen that others should learn, at least vicariously, similar lessons for the work of pastoring,

---

[10]   This contrasts with the academic prizing of detachment –*apatheia* rather than *empatheia*.

[11]   Collingwood, *Ruskin Cross*, p. 2.

[12]   Jeffrey L. Spear, 'Ruskin as a Prejudiced Reader', *English Literary History*, 49 (1982): 73–98, at p. 75. See Chapter 2, p. 25.

and in expressing this he turned the language of interpretation and hermeneutics to include living human beings as well as written texts. In doing this he bequeathed an explanatory and imaginative concept of great richness to subsequent pastoral, practical and public theology. To trace the use and development of this would require a book in itself but in particular Donald Capps picked up and expounded this concept, and Bonnie Miller-McLemore has developed it to embrace a more communal paradigm as the 'living human web'.[13] It has been and still is a foundational concept in pastoral theology.

Biblical hermeneutics and practical theology thus lie within the same stream of ideas and practices, and it is a stream in which John Ruskin was at home. The discussions of both biblical interpretation and the interpretation of human situations as practised in the discipline of practical theology are held within a wider discussion of the nature of interpretation itself. This in principle makes an exploration of the Bible and practical theology a possible, necessary and potentially fruitful one. I would, however, like to raise some problems in relation to a too easy acceptance both of some biblical interpretative strategies and of the foundational image of the 'living human document', which elide the reading and interpretation of a text with the reading and interpretation of human beings. There are some important differences between interpreting a text and interpreting a human being.

Texts and People are not the Same: the 'Living Human Document' Revisited

A basic assumption in the tradition of interpretation I have described is that the text, or a person, is an 'Other' over against which we stand. Towards this Other we must make two movements, the first of which is seeing the distinction between the two horizons: the Other's horizon or the historical horizon, and our horizon or the contemporary horizon. Then we recognise some sort of relationship between the horizons, which expands our initial position. This is sometimes thought of, though contestedly, as a 'fusion' of horizons. Anthony Thiselton has been a key exponent in a British context of this tradition in biblical hermeneutics and his position is well summed up in his Preface to the new edition of *New Horizons in Hermeneutics: The Theory and Practice of Transforming Bible Reading*:

---

13   Donald Capps, *Pastoral Care and Hermeneutics* (Philadelphia: Fortress Press, 1984); Bonnie J. Miller-McLemore, 'The Living Human Web: Pastoral Theology at the Turn of the Century', in Jeanne Stevenson Moessner (ed.), *Through the Eyes of Women: Insights for Pastoral Care* (Minneapolis: Fortress Press, 1996), pp. 9–26; for Boisen, see Daniel S. Shipani, 'Case Study Method', in Bonnie J. Miller-McLemore (ed.), *The Wiley-Blackwell Companion to Practical Theology* (Oxford: Wiley-Blackwell, 2011), pp. 91–101, at p. 93; Edward Farley has offered a concise account of interpreting situations in his essay of that title: Edward Farley, 'Interpreting Situations: An Inquiry into the Nature of Practical Theology', in James Woodward and Stephen Pattison (eds), *The Blackwell Reader in Pastoral and Practical Theology* (Oxford: Blackwell, 2000), pp. 135–45.

First, as its sub-title indicates, my concern in *New Horizons* is not only to *engage* with the horizons of the text, but also to explore *the transforming effects of the Bible*. It is clear throughout my argument that the Bible is given not primarily as an encyclopaedia of information on all subjects, but as a source of *transformation, to shape readers* in accordance with God's purpose for them ... Biblical texts deliver us from self-preoccupation or self-centredness, as we open ourselves to what is 'Other', 'Beyond', or to the voice of God.[14]

In this movement, in both biblical hermeneutics and practical theological hermeneutics, self-understanding is crucial. So far there is similarity between interpreting a written text and interpreting the living human document.

In interpreting both texts and human beings we inevitably build constructions of them. In the humanistic tradition of hermeneutics under discussion there is an attempt to understand that which is 'Other', an attempt in which we strive to control our understanding in authentic response to the sign-signals we receive from the Other. We should not impose meaning but wrestle with what they are trying to 'say' to us.[15]

I would, however, like to suggest that there is a radical distinction between the living human being who can enter into a dialogue and answer us back, and the text, which cannot, at least in any straightforward sense. This is an important and disputed claim and needs to be teased out further. First, texts are a kind of trace of the human, footprints left behind. Written texts are not the only such traces human beings leave. The huge stones at Men ar Rompet are traces, as are most objects in museums – tools, clothing, coins and weapons. As Neil MacGregor said of the Hornedjitef Mummy he examined in the first broadcast of his 'A History of the World in 100 Objects': 'he is his own document'.[16] But our access to the author of the document forever remains a mystery. We can tentatively explore, intuit and resonate with his document, but who and how he was is forever veiled from our grasp. Architecture, music and art are also 'traces' human beings imprint in the world for others to see and understand – or not. But none of these are the living human being itself. In conversation with another human being I can be answered back, corrected in my understanding, deliberately or in passing, in ways that are direct, unlike the corrections that have an impact on me as a result of my reading, as I seek to reconstruct meaning from the traces of the human. I have a vivid

---

[14]   Thiselton, *New Horizons*, p. xv.

[15]   There are more recent understandings of interpretation and reading, less concerned, if at all, with anything other than our own responses and constructions, which are seen as a free-standing 'play', not to be controlled by any authorial intent, historical objectivity or humanistic sympathy between reader and text/author. For an overall introduction to the range of contemporary discussion in biblical hermeneutics, see Holgate and Starr, *SCM Study Guide* or Oeming, *Contemporary Biblical Hermeneutics*.

[16]   Neil MacGregor, *The History of the World in 100 Objects* (London: Penguin, 2012), p. 4.

example before me every week as I talk with a student from a different culture from myself, whose writing I find particularly dense. Painstakingly, we struggle through question and answer for an hour, backwards and forwards, until I gain more clarity. Understanding a human being is not easy, nor does it have guaranteed success. It does, however, have an element of mutual dialogue which the coming to an understanding of texts or any other 'traces left behind' does not.

The 'Human Form Divine'

There is a particular issue to attend to here in terms of biblical hermeneutics. For the Christian reader at least, a key function of the Bible is to render a person to us – Jesus Christ. Furthermore, this person, Jesus Christ, in his life and work, in his death and resurrection, is not presented to us to confirm us in our beliefs and our practices, but to challenge them. We can build any imaginary world we choose. Indeed, we do this, as the history of 'life of Jesus' research has shown – 'The Christ that Harnack saw, looking back through nineteen centuries of Catholic darkness, is only the reflection of a Liberal Protestant face, seen at the bottom of a deep well.'[17] The difficult question is *how* we can allow that which is Other, supremely Jesus, to surprise us, to question and challenge us, when our primary access is textual, and consists in an account of the traces, the *vestigia*, he left behind? I write 'primary' because a key element of the way in which the New Testament portrays Jesus is the fact that such encounters are also 'extra-textual': 'in as much as you have done it to one of the least of these you have done it to me' (Matt. 25.40).

In my own earlier work I contended that there are four 'texts' for practical theology, of which God is one, in an analogous sense.[18] I would now want to make a distinction between *vestigial* texts, for example written texts – the texts of the Christian tradition and of the secular world – and those 'texts' that are living and personal, the 'living human document'.

There is a significant difference between a vestigial, trace-like, text and the living person who leaves the trace. The primary living and personal 'texts' are human. Augustine contends that the world is full of the *vestigia*, the traces, of the Trinity. Furthermore there is a classical distinction made between the *essential* Trinity – God as God is in Godself – and the *economic* Trinity – God as God is and appears in self-disposal towards the world.[19] Both of these ideas point towards the sense I am groping for – the possibility of perceiving God within the world and

---

[17]   George Tyrrell, *Christianity at the Crossroads* (London: Longmans, Green, 1910), p. 44.

[18]   Zoë Bennett Moore, 'Pastoral Theology as Hermeneutics', *British Journal of Theological Education*, 12.1 (2001): 7–18.

[19]   For an exploration of these ideas in the context of practical theology, see Neil Pembroke, *Renewing Pastoral Practice: Trinitarian Perspectives on Pastoral Care and Counselling* (Aldershot: Ashgate, 2006), pp. 11–12, 14.

our experience, through these *vestigia*. That is the way to understand Christianity's fundamental claim that human beings can have a relationship with God of an 'I-thou' character not just an 'I-it' character. This I-thou is possible through the Spirit, which/who lifts the relationship between humans and God from the examination of 'traces' to a relationship analogous to a human-to-human relationship:

> These things God has revealed to us through the Spirit; for the Spirit searches everything, even the depths of God. For what human being knows what is truly human except the human spirit that is within? So no one comprehends what is truly God's except the Spirit of God. Now we have received not the spirit of the world, but the Spirit that is from God, so that we may understand the gifts bestowed on us by God. (1 Cor. 2.11–12)

This is a wonderful description of heart-sight; of the personal connectedness that is the basis of hermeneutics, of texts and traces and supremely of the human; and of how understanding and interpretation of God might be possible. But, as Paul continually reminds his readers throughout 1 Corinthians, that understanding comes primarily through engagement with fellow human beings, manifesting faith, hope and love. That is where the presence of God is to be found (1 Cor. 3.16; 6.19).

Speaking of the Spirit prompts a return to the question raised earlier of the rendering of the person of Jesus Christ to us. He is accessible, Christians believe, not only through texts (supremely the Bible) but also through the Spirit. Historical life of Jesus research is forever inconclusive and partial, inclined to find Jesus in our own image. The discrediting of the nineteenth-century version of such a quest and the rediscovery of the 'eschatological Jesus', who was thought by many to be an embarrassment for the modern world, set in train a tension, one pole of which is expressed in Albert Schweitzer's famous words that conclude his magisterial *Quest for the Historical Jesus*:

> He comes to us as One unknown, without a name, as of old, by the lake side, He came to those men who knew Him not. He speaks to us the same word: 'Follow thou me!' and sets us to the tasks which He has to fulfill for our time. He commands. And to those who obey Him, whether they be wise or simple, He will reveal Himself in the toils, the conflicts, the sufferings which they shall pass through in His fellowship, and, as an ineffable mystery, they shall learn in their own experience Who He is.[20]

Here the emphasis is on revelation and on experience, the seeing of the heart, through which we may come to know Christ. Of course this move too may easily recreate Christ in our own image, as that which we see, or He whom we see coming

---

[20]   Albert Schweitzer, *The Quest of the Historical Jesus: A Critical Study of its Progress from Reimarus to Wrede*, with a preface by F.C. Burkitt, 2nd English edn, tr. W. Montgomery (London: A & C Black, 1911), p. 401.

to us along the lake may be made in our own image. Much of the contention between those two traditions I identified in Chapter 3 lies in a discussion about whether starting with the texts of the tradition or starting with the experiential is more likely to produce an ideological distortion in our seeing, our heart-sight, of those particular Others we name as Jesus Christ and as God: and there are perils in both ways.

Chapter 8

On Prophetic Seeing

The Prophet

The phrase 'prophet of doom' is typical of the way in which we think about prophecy; it is about the prediction of disaster. But in addition to such 'foretelling', there is also 'forth telling' (pronouncing on the state of society and individuals), albeit often with the threat of judgment and a message of hope. That speaking about how things are is central to biblical prophecy. Amos, Isaiah, Jeremiah and Hosea all criticised the social situation of their context and urged change to avoid disaster (Amos 5.10–15). It was and is open to anyone who saw what was amiss and spoke about the injustice to fulfil this role (Amos 7.14–15). William Blake put it well in words that encapsulate much of what Ruskin was about: 'Every honest man is a Prophet; he utters his opinion both of private & public matters. Thus: If you go on So, the result is So.'[1]

While it is true that some form of communication – be it speaking, writing or acting out (as Ezekiel) – is also part of the prophetic task, and the next section will examine this, for now it is *seeing* that concerns us. The prophet is often known as the 'seer', one who sees visions, the one who sees contemporary events in God's light, with a penetrating truth. Think of Amos and his plumb line, the vision in which he saw God in the midst of contemporary life, measuring it and judging it; or of John of Patmos, seeing spread out before his eyes the visions of destruction, of courageous witness and of heavenly glory and hope, moving between heaven and earth, indeed seeing heaven and earth in one vision, with their truths overlaid upon one another, seeing the veil drawn back, the revealing, 'apocalyptic' vision.[2]

For example, in 2 Kings 6 Elisha the man of God, surrounded by the horses and chariots of the king of Aram, and faced by the terror of his servant, prays: 'Lord please open his eyes that he may see' (2 Kings 6.17). The servant's eyes are opened, and he sees the mountain full of the horses and chariots of the Lord, way outnumbering those of the king of Aram, encompassing them. The prophet sees the truth, and prays that God may draw back the veil for others as he speaks it. Good seeing and courageous speaking may enable good seeing in others.

---

[1]   From Blake's marginal annotations to Richard Watson's 'Apology', 14, in W. Blake, *Blake: Complete Writings*, ed. G. Keynes (Oxford: Oxford University Press, 1966), p. 392.

[2]   Amos 7.7–9; Revelation.

This cameo illustrates beautifully the need to have one eye on the contemporary situation and one eye on the reality as seen through our understanding of God. Furthermore it illustrates the inappropriateness of using the categories whereby we understand biblical matters – here prophecy and apocalyptic – in too watertight compartments.[3] The same could be said of wisdom and prophecy. We are, rightly, used to following the traditional distinction between the prophetic books in the Bible and the Wisdom literature. However, in practice there is much overlap. Ruskin is depicted, insightfully, by Michael Wheeler as a 'Victorian Solomon', drawing inspiration for what he said and the manner of his saying from that biblical dispenser of wisdom, and wanting to teach people how to live, 'challeng[ing] late Victorian society to respond to his version of apocalyptic wisdom'.[4] Stuart Eagles, on the other hand, in the title of his book calls Ruskin a 'Victorian prophet', attacking contemporary realities in the name of deeper and truer perceptions of human values under God.[5] Sage, prophet and apocalyptic seer are all apt descriptions of this man who was shaped in his very being by the biblical text.

There was a price to pay. '[M]y word ... shall not return to me empty', says the Lord through the prophet Isaiah.[6] The prophet, however, often feels that his words do return empty. Ruskin's social critique in *Unto this Last* was derided as the preaching of a mad governess.[7] A guest who shared dinner with Ruskin at Hawarden with Gladstone in 1878 recalled, 'an utter hopelessness; a real, pure despair beneath the sunlight of his smile, and ringing through all he said. Why it does not wholly paralyse him I cannot make out.'[8] In this he repeats the judgment of Henry James who 10 years earlier saw Ruskin as 'weakness, pure and simple' and 'scared back by the grim face of reality'.[9] Prophetic seeing requires an attention to grim reality, and prophetic telling usually brings loneliness and public criticism. The prophet is one who *is*, one whose whole being before God holds God's word to us, and whom the telling forth of that word will agonise and consume and ultimately transfigure. Like Moses, the prophet is often one who is rejected not only by those he condemns but by his own people. Alfred de Vigny's poem, in which he pictures Moses standing alone on the mountain, facing the promised land, facing his death and facing God, encapsulates for us 'the prophet': Lord I have lived powerful and alone, let me sleep now.[10] Some of the loneliness and the personal agony of de Vigny's Moses was Ruskin's lot also.

---

[3]   See Christopher Rowland, *The Open Heaven: A Study of Apocalyptic in Judaism and Early Christianity* (London: SPCK, 1982), p. 70.

[4]   Wheeler, *Ruskin's God*, p. xv.

[5]   Eagles, *After Ruskin: The Social and Political Legacies of a Victorian Prophet*.

[6]   Isaiah 55.11.

[7]   *Works*, 17, xxviii, note the sexist and anti-religious tone.

[8]   Quoted in Hilton, *John Ruskin*, p. 651.

[9]   Quoted in Hilton, *John Ruskin*, p. 435.

[10]   'O Seigneur! J'ai vécu puissant et solitaire./ Laissez-moi m'endormir du sommeil de la terre!' Alfred de Vigny, *Möise*, in *The Oxford Book of French Verse, XIIIth–XIXth*

'The Work of Iron'

In 1858 Ruskin was invited, as eminent professors often were (he was then Slade Professor of Fine Art in the University of Oxford) to give a public lecture for the edification of the middle classes, in this case for the good people of Tunbridge Wells. Inviting Ruskin was always dangerous, because he would turn the occasion into a disquisition on the evils of industrial Britain and, specifically, his audience's complicity in this. This was no exception, and talk of the aesthetic properties of the glowing warm colour of the iron in their famous chalybeate spring turned to the moral challenges posed by the uses of iron in war and for producing pointless and ugly artefacts. Ruskin then drew from his internal arsenal of biblical texts a barrage of exhortations and judgments, mainly from the Psalms, on those who in making themselves rich oppressed, ate up and murdered the poor. He expressly points out that he is speaking, he is sure, to regular attenders of the Church of England, who must hear these words over and over again in church but never see that they are speaking to *them*.[11]

Iron railings particularly drew his ire; he regarded them as aesthetically appalling and socially destructive. In 1866 in *The Crown of Wild Olive* (four lectures on industry and war) he wrote of how he walked through the backstreets of Croydon and passed a new public-house. In front of it was a space of about two feet between the building and the pavement which the owner sought to enhance by fencing it

> from the pavement by an imposing iron railing, having four or five spear-heads to the yard of it, and six feet high; containing as much iron and iron-work, indeed, as could well be put into the space; and by this stately arrangement, the little piece of dead ground within, between wall and street, became a protective receptacle of refuse; cigar ends, and oyster shells, and the like, such as an open-handed English street populace habitually scatters; and was thus left, unsweepable by any ordinary methods.[12]

'What Ruskin's physical eyes have acutely observed his inner eyes examine further. He notes that iron railings are ugly, the litter pestilent, and the work in the iron foundry fatally dangerous.'[13] To illustrate this he instances a recent fatal accident in a blast furnace in Wolverhampton, noting that the only reason that 'the strength and life of the English operative were spent in defiling ground, instead of redeeming it' is that 'the capitalist can charge per-centage on the work in one case,

---

Century, chosen by St John Lucas (Oxford: Clarendon Press, 1907), p. 293.

[11]   *Works*, 16, 396–7.

[12]   *Works*, 18, 387.

[13]   Zoë Bennett, '"To be taught to see is to gain word and thought at once": John Ruskin and Practical Theology', *Practical Theology*, 1.1 (2008): 85–93, at 86.

and cannot in the other'.[14] Here we have an example of the 'pastoral cycle' at work – observation, analysis, the bringing into dialogue with the Christian tradition, and the move into renewed and changed action.

An important distinction needs to be made here between two quite different uses of the pastoral cycle, which are often confused in practical theology. The origins of the modern use of the action/reflection cycle, which is so deeply a part of contemporary public practical theology, are twofold. The first is in liberation theology, where praxis involves the constant dialectic between action and reflection, and experience and the contemporary situation are interrogated and analysed, in order to understand it better and through that understanding to move intentionally towards more informed action. The intention in this tradition is social change and transformation, for the benefit of the poorest and least in society.[15] The second origin is in the professional reflective practice movement, deriving from the work of Donald Schön in reflection 'on' and 'in' practice, and from David Kolb's experiential learning cycle.[16] This, as it is put to work in contemporary society, is more about professional effectiveness than about social transformation and may be made to serve a quite conservative agenda of cost-cutting and performance targets within the market economy. Clearly the first of these is central to prophetic seeing; the second may sometimes be inimical to it.

Prophetic seeing, as exemplified by Ruskin's observation of the work of iron in our society, or in liberation theology's use of the pastoral cycle, is *connective*, it is imaginative, it is compassionate and it is critical. Ruskin makes the connection between the iron he sees on the street and the work which went into making it, between the conditions of that work and the injunctions of the Psalms. To work out some of the realities of those connections is an analytical task, requiring sociological, theological and hermeneutical understanding, and the results are always open to questioning and refutation. That he made the connections, trusted his values and intuitions and defended them in the face of ridicule is a mark of Ruskin's stature. This example from Ruskin's prophetic seeing reveals an important aspect of the pastoral cycle. It is often asked why the phase of sociological analysis should precede that of bringing to bear the Christian tradition on the subject. It is not a matter of giving sociological analysis more importance; it is a matter of procedural priority, since the question is, *what is the subject matter* with which the Christian tradition is brought into engagement? Is it iron railings and litter? Or is it the political and economic principles and practices that cause there to be fatally dangerous working conditions and rubbish in the streets? It is the latter on which

---

[14]   *Works*, 18, 388.

[15]   Leonardo Boff and Clodovis Boff, *Introducing Liberation Theology*, trans. Paul Burns (Maryknoll, NY: Orbis Books, 1987).

[16]   Donald Schön, *The Reflective Practitioner: How Professionals Think in Action* (Aldershot: Ashgate, 2003; originally published London: Maurice Temple Smith, 1983); David Kolb, *Experiential Learning: Experience as the Source of Learning and Development* (Englewood Cliffs, NJ: Prentice Hall, 1984).

the prophetic imagination is brought to bear, and to arrive at the latter is the wo... of sociological analysis.[17]

Such work is secondly *imaginative*. The connections are not only or even initially logical. They require that Ruskin digs beneath what is seen on the surface – that the litter puts him in mind of the street sweepers, the wrought iron of the factory accident, the industrial conditions of the Psalmist's denunciations. Here we have the process delineated in Chapter 5 in which by a hermeneutic of immediacy and of analogy two things are 'seen' together and connections made imaginatively and comparatively. There the text of the Bible and the text of the world were juxtaposed; here we see that method extended as the iron railings with the litter behind them set off a whole train of imaginative as well as analytical processes in Ruskin in the service of his prophetic denunciation of the contemporary political economy. The one illuminates the other. You cannot understand the Psalms without the attentive seeing of what is going on, but you notice what is going on because of the repeated denunciation of the oppression of the poor. As in Isaiah 6.9, you can see without understanding; what is crucial is seeing with understanding. That comes via the dialectic between experience and the strange world of the Bible.

Prophetic seeing is *compassionate*. Ruskin has read of the accident in the foundry where the young men were burned to death and it has stayed with him and moved him. He cares that people waste their time in useless occupation which brings no life, and in dangerous occupation which brings death. He sees the iron railings, as he has read the newspaper account, with heart-sight. It is this heart-sight that motivates and drives him, but crucially not just on a mission but with a vision. Compassion enables him to see better as it opens up the imagination to work on the initial clarity and precision of his observation.

Finally, prophetic seeing is also *critical* – critical not only of the social-economic status quo in which human beings are degraded, but also of established religion, in which respectable churchgoers hear the Psalms Sunday by Sunday and never dream that their accusations are meant for them. Here Ruskin stands in the tradition of biblical prophecy, in which from the core of the faith in its obedience and righteousness towards God – one and the same thing as compassion and justice in human relationships – social and religious practices are subjected to criticism.

Journeying Diaries

Prophetic seeing applies to the way we see the Bible as well as to the way we see society and its artefacts around us. I mentioned in Chapter 5 the material from Ruskin's diaries of 1858/1859 at the time of his 'unconversion'. This was very much part of a process of internalisation of belief rather than a sudden change

---

[17]   Clodovis Boff makes a classical statement of this position for liberation theology in *Theology and Praxis*. for which see Bennett, 'Praxis-based Epistemology'.

of heart.[18] There are several aspects of the context of these diary notes that are instructive and inspirational for the kind of seeing of religious tradition that enables prophecy. First, they shows us a man at a crisis point, a *kairos*, in his life, turning to the Bible and agonising over the meaning of those passages in which he knew lay the stuff that he had to come to terms with – the gospels and particularly the first five chapters of Romans, so important to the evangelical faith he was leaving behind as well as to an understanding of the meaning of divine justice.

These diary pages show us the Bible in the midst of a man's daily life; they are truly journeying diaries. On the right-hand page is a travelogue – a list of the places visited on this last continental journey Ruskin took with his parents. On the left are the notes on Romans. The book went with him each day, embedded in his European travels, and embedded in his journey of faith.[19]

Foremost among the features of Ruskin's prophetic seeing is his determination to see through to the ways of God in the text. He wrestled to find what some critics call 'die Sache' of the text, the real stuff, the heart of its message.[20] He struggled with other people's interpretations of the text, with that which had been handed down to him by his tradition. He struggled with all this in the light of what he saw in the world around him and of what he could internalise in his own relationship with God.

In his seeing of the Bible Ruskin was nothing if not persistent. This is a characteristic of prophetic seeing – dogged persistence in the struggle to make sense of inherited faith. For example, commenting on the Temptation story and what is meant by 'everything which comes out of the mouth of God', he reviews his own repeated failure to understand, 'After all, the more I think the more puzzled I become;– I suppose this was the way I lost understanding of the words before.' But he doesn't give up, either on the specific details or on the big questions, such as the meaning of 'the obedience of faith' – in Romans 1.5. This last is so important to him from his evangelical background. Coming to an understanding of faith and works belonging together, and together standing as the opposite of fear, he is able

---

[18] Robert Hewison, *Ruskin on Venice* (New Haven and London: Yale University Press, 2009), pp. 248–50.

[19] These sections are found in RF MS 11, Ruskin Foundation (Ruskin Library, Lancaster University). They begin on folio 31 and continue with extensive page breaks. The material on folios 31–2, 107, 111, 116–17, 125, 163–71B comments mainly on Matthew's Gospel and was begun in Baveno in July 1858. Folio 106 has further comment on what he has earlier written – 'Dresden Sunday 26th June 59. Comments, written on the passage opposite, a year afterwards'. The material on folios 283–301 (continuous) starts with Galatians 1.4 but quickly moves on to an extended discussion of the early chapters of Paul's letter to the Romans. It begins on Sunday, 7 August in Baden and ends with the words 'Ends journey of 1859'. See Bennett, '"A fact full of power"'.

[20] Robert Morgan, '*Sachkritik* in Reception History', *Journal for the Study of the New Testament*, 33 (December 2010): 175–90.

to move forward into his prophetic critique, in which he calls for both faith and works, in spite of much that would make him fear.[21]

A further characteristic of Ruskin's work in these diaries is a meticulous attention to detail. The grand canvas painting of Ruskin's prophetic seeing of the Bible – the huge themes such as justice, fatherly providence, community and the place of money – is undergirded by that 'bird's eye' vision in which each blade of grass is examined particularly.[22] He cares how words are translated, like justice not righteousness for *dikaiosune* or 'Note respecting conversion. If people would only say turned instead of converted – how much trouble it would save. That wretchedly misunderstood verb.' He pores over the meaning of words, fuelling his prophetic passion with precision of exegesis.[23]

See and Tell

'To see something and to tell what it saw in a plain way': thus Ruskin sums up the greatest thing a human soul ever does. Section 2 has primarily explored the 'seeing' element. Using John Ruskin as an inspiration and an example we have looked at seeing clearly, at seeing with the heart and at prophetic seeing. This has inevitably involved also attention to clear-sighted, passionate and prophetic 'telling'. The next section of this book moves on to contemporary seeing and telling. It explores how we form texts that tell what we have seen: texts that engage, yes the Bible, yes the contemporary reality, yes an analysis of that reality – but more even than all of these, texts that engage the audience, the hearer or the reader, texts that communicate and persuade, texts that do work in the public square.

---

[21]   See a similar interpretation in Ernst Käsemann, *Commentary on Romans*, trans. and ed. G.W. Bromiley (London: SCM Press, 1980).

[22]   See Drury, 'Ruskin's Way', and this book Chapter 6, pp. 82, 87.

[23]   By using the word *exegesis* I am not meaning to contradict all I said in Part I and suggest this process is a neutral or 'objective' one for Ruskin any more than for anyone else.

PART III
The Bible and Theology in the Public Sphere

Central to this book thus far has been the idea that there are two 'texts' with which we engage when doing practical and public theology: the texts of the tradition and the texts of experience, or, as liberation theology has it, the text of the Bible and the 'text of life'. Both kinds of texts require that we see them well in order to interpret them. Thus far we have concentrated on the seeing of these 'texts', on the understanding of them and their contextualisation, and also on their mutual relations and respective importance.

Seeing clearly is the first movement in practical and public theology. Such seeing of the text of life involves both sight and, crucially, insight: the attentive precision of detailed observation, the engagement of the heart and the imagination, and the courageous contextualisation of our seeing within public and private struggles. Seeing well as practical or public theologians means more than receiving images on a mental retina; it means interpretation of those images to name them, and interpretation of those images by acts of comparison, of excavation, of imaginative engagement and of evaluation to discern – to discern the meaning of faithful living in our times.

This book is concerned with the complexities of bringing together different worlds. Such a dialectic constitutes its heartbeat. This enterprise, which lies at the core of biblical hermeneutics, also animates and shapes practical and public theology, which is interested in the production of texts, which have their own life once they are created. The texts of public theology can themselves be put on the map of the three worlds – author, reader and text.

We have considered how John Ruskin, a man of the Victorian era and right at the heart of questions of authority in church and society, and of historical and scientific consciousness, dealt personally with the Bible and used it in the public texts he produced. The ultimate goal of the book is not solely the examination of others' texts but the opening up of possibilities for the reader's own use of the Bible in a public context. So, Part III of the book will involve the examination of the use of the Bible in contemporary texts of public theology.

The choice of the first two texts to examine in this part has been determined initially by variety – one long deliberated, the other 'of the occasion'; one communally written, the other an interview with an individual in the midst of a controversial piece of direct action; one of more domestic interest, the other international; each displaying different characteristics of Christian use of the Bible in the midst of the text of life; both connected to action. They also offer contrasting hermeneutical perspectives, one in which the Bible functions spontaneously and more intuitively, the other where the role of the Bible is understood within a tradition of hermeneutical engagement as well as communal reflection.

The book ends as it began, with the autobiographical. The context of seeing and understanding – both of the text of the Bible and of the text of life – is performance, and critical reflection on that performance. My final chapter allows me to enact something of the core message of this book, which is the need for self-reflexivity. Neither Ruskin, as a historical perspective, nor either of the contemporary perspectives I have chosen to examine in detail offer a blueprint of how to use the Bible in public theology. We are in every case left with a hermeneutical deficit. The invitation of the book is to examine our own practice, and what it offers is some tools with which to do this and some perspectives from which to see ourselves.

Chapter 9
A Resignation and an Interview: The Bible and Corporate Finance

Seeing the text of the Bible is always done in the context of the text of life, whether that life is lived in the rarefied world of the academy or on the streets. To say of the Bible that it is for all times, people and places is to say that in each new context the lines making connections between the Bible and contemporary human life will be specific to that context, to that slice of life.

That 'seeing', which is directed to the text of the Bible and to the text of life, and to their mutual interpretation, has furnished the material for Parts I and II of this book. In Part III I move on to introduce a third text, and that third text is always in the context of what might be seen as a fourth. It would be helpful to set them out:

- the text of life – seeing
- the text of the Bible – seeing
- the reflective text – telling
- the performed text – acting, into which the ongoing activity of others is also invited.

This fourth 'text' is in fact part of the first, the text of life. It is where we get to at the end of the pastoral 'spiral' as action is renewed.

That good seeing, which attends to the multiplicity of presented details and which penetrates beneath the surface in interpretation and judgment, is for practical theology only the beginning of the task. The next step is often conceived within the pastoral reflective cycle as the task of acting, thus creating a spiral of seeing, judging and acting, leading to fresh seeing brought about by new action and thus an ongoing process. Action is indeed a, if not *the*, primary element in practical theology, as the generator of 'seeing', and in a dialectical relationship to it. However, to conceive the matter thus is to leave out a critically important element of public theology – the task of telling. The concentration on the cycle of action/reflection within practical, and thus public, theology has distracted from our attending to *how* the fruits of our theological reflection are presented in the public domain. Public presentation of what we have 'seen', in spoken and written word, but also in other media, may be the catalyst for action by others, which is a vital element of practical and public theology.

> [T]he greatest thing a human soul ever does in this world is to *see* something, and tell what it saw in a plain way.[1]

These two activities, seeing clearly and telling what you saw in a plain way, are at the heart of what it means to be a practical and public theologian. The act of telling produces a third text, the reflective text, in which what you have 'seen' is mediated. It may be written in a book, a newspaper or a verbatim. It may be written in a poem, or indeed it may take its form as a film, a piece of music, a play or an artwork. But it is *'told'*. The fruits of our seeing and reflection must find a 'reflective text' in order to find a public.

The final step – the action and performance required by our texts, forming thus a further text – is not neglected by Ruskin. His life was full of the performance of his texts, from his public lectures to the work of St George's Guild. But the verbal articulation of the need for this fourth text is put classically by an older historical figure, the radical Digger Gerrard Winstanley (1609–76): 'I have Writ, I have Acted, I have Peace', he wrote in one of his last works. For Winstanley it was 'action', putting his spade into the soil at St George's Hill and digging, that was the 'life of all' next to which 'words and writings must die'; and yet his writing was also crucially related to his action and began to emerge from it – witnessing and calling others to action and defending what he and his companions were doing in digging the common land.[2] Thus while these three chapters in Part III address the reflective texts that do work in the public sphere, such texts should be seen within a context: that writing or other public communication of the message is only one element within a wider practical and activist commitment to practice and action.

The moment of telling, of prophecy in word, drama, music or art, is a crucial moment in the cycle of public transformation. In practical theology it is often forgotten that we do not only see and read texts, we produce them, and for the work of public theology this is no less an important task. The function of such texts is intended to be performative, to persuade others of the truth of what we have seen and of the importance of acting on it.

The shape and form, the crafted and performative passion of the chosen medium is vital to the work of public theology. It returns us to the text of life, as the textured action, the performance, arises out of and in conjunction with all the other texts. Such a text has been described as a 'performance' of the Bible itself, or as acting out an as yet unfinished final act of a play.[3] It is, however, more than that. It is the

---

[1] Ruskin, *Works*, 5, 333.

[2] Corns, Hughes and Loewenstein (eds), *Complete Works of Gerrard Winstanley*, vol. 2, pp. 149 and 80.

[3] Nicholas Lash, 'Performing the Scriptures', in *Theology on the Way to Emmaus* (London: SCM Press, 1986), pp. 37–46; Christopher Rowland and John Roberts, *The Bible*

actions performed by individuals and by the community which in themselves invite others into further action, sometimes over a long period of time. It is 'keeping faith in practice'.[4] It is also experimentation, risking and daring, trying out and then reflecting. The reflective moment is essential – both to the acting and to the understanding and interpretation – both of the Bible and of the practices of life.

Features of the reflective text, the presentation of theological reflection on the text of life and the text of the Bible, as is found in Ruskin's work, are that it is:

- rooted in the contemporary context
- drawn from the Christian heritage and tradition, especially the Bible
- personal and public
- carefully and creatively crafted
- performed and performative.

This last leads into consideration of the enacted text.

The remainder of Part III will examine three different contemporary texts. In so doing it will make use of these features of Ruskin's work which have been displayed throughout Part II. The problematic laid out in Part I is revisited in the light of what has been learned from the historical consideration of Ruskin, through an examination of contemporary texts that involve the bringing together of the Bible and life. The first of these is a newspaper interview concerning a high profile resignation and global financial issues, the second an ecumenical church document concerning the Israel/Palestine question, and the third a personal text reflecting on a British Higher Education programme. The emphasis throughout will be on observation and evaluation of the use of the Bible.

Occupy London Stock Exchange and St Paul's Cathedral – October 2011

During October 2011, as part of a global movement, Occupy London set up camp outside St Paul's Cathedral, in the space jointly owned by St Paul's and the Corporation of London. Describing itself as a peaceful and non-hierarchical forum, the Occupy movement sought to promote public debate, to think outside the box and to create alternatives to the existing undemocratic and unjust financial system.

> **Occupy London** stands together with occupations all over the world; we are the 99%. We are a peaceful non-hierarchical forum. **We're in agreement that the current system is undemocratic and unjust**. We need alternatives; you are invited to join us in debate and developing them; to create a better future for everyone.[5]

for Sinners: Interpretation in the Present Time (London: SPCK, 2008), pp. 6–8, with reference to Tom Wright, 'How Can the Bible be Authoritative?', *Vox Evangelica*, 21 (1991): 7–32.

[4] Sweeney et al., *Keeping Faith.*
[5] http://occupylsx.org/ (accessed 07.11.11).

Initially the clerical authorities of St Paul's Cathedral refused to talk with the people in the camp, shut the Cathedral to the public for the first time since the Second World War, on alleged health and safety grounds, and made it clear that they would join with the Corporation of London in having the demonstrators moved on. This would have inevitably involved violence. The Canon Chancellor of St Paul's resigned.

Giles Fraser was not only Canon Chancellor but also headed up the St Paul's Institute, which describes itself as 'part of the wider mission of St Paul's Cathedral', designed to challenge and to educate, and to 'bring finance and economics into dialogue with Christian ethics and theology', on whose website the then Archbishop of Canterbury Rowan Williams wrote:

> An ethical approach to economics requires us to move away from the illusion
> that economics can be considered separately from questions of the health and
> well-being of the society we inhabit.[6]

It seemed to Giles Fraser, and to much public opinion, that to refuse to talk to the Occupy London camp and to have them forcibly moved on by the police was not to fulfil the church's or his own role's mission.

This incident created many 'texts' in the national newspapers. In particular I want here to look at a text created in *The Guardian* of 28 October 2011 in which Giles Fraser gave an interview to Alan Rusbridger. This text covered one and a half adjacent pages of the broadsheet and was headed 'A Troublesome Priest? I Get Fitted Up as Wat Tyler, But I'm No Radical'. There was a large picture of Fraser looking thoughtful in open-necked shirt and jacket. One of the two quotation 'bites' picked out in large bold was: 'Money is the No 1 moral issue in the Bible, but how many sermons do you get about that? Very few.' On the same page a large bold type quotation from Fraser, in a separate article spilling over from page 1 read, 'I could imagine Jesus being born in the camp.'[7]

This text was unusual and interesting as a 'text of theological reflection' – which it clearly was. First it was not actually written by the reflector himself, but by an interviewer; the 'text' Giles Fraser gave was a verbal one, and a responsive one. Second, it was created in the heat of the moment, under serious public and private pressure. One might say that Fraser's reflections were more like what Donald Schön calls 'reflection *in* action' than 'reflection *on* action'.[8] He hardly had a chance to reflect before he was asked to speak, and his words should be seen in that light. While they were not strictly speaking reflection while actually engaged in an action, they were certainly reflection in the midst of a series of actions.

---

6   http://www.stpaulsinstitute.org.uk/Mission (accessed 14.11.11).

7   Alan Rusbridger, 'A Troublesome Priest? I Get Fitted Up as Wat Tyler, But I'm No Radical', interview with Rev Dr Giles Fraser, *The Guardian*, Friday, 28 October 2011, pp. 16–17.

8   Schön, *The Reflective Practitioner*, pp. 61–2.

Rooted in the Contemporary World

To say this material was rooted in the contemporary world is to state the utterly obvious. This piece was in a national daily newspaper, commenting on the events that were reported on the front page of that and other papers. It concerned not only the capital city and the cathedral that was repeatedly described as emblem of the city, emphasising its survival through the Battle of Britain and its geographical positioning in the financial heart of London, but also the central national and global contemporary issue – finance, the banks, the economy. The incident concerned a serious attempt by citizens of the UK, and all over the world, to speak and act prophetically in favour of social justice and of values alternative to Mammon (the biblical word was used in public discussion). What was happening was happening daily on our television screens in front of our eyes.

Drawn from the Christian Heritage

This text is soaked in the Christian tradition – from its title invoking Thomas à Becket and Wat Tyler, to its opening and closing pictures of Fraser the priest 'in the shadow of Wren's cathedral', and most significantly of all Fraser's own repeated invocations of Jesus and of the Bible.

Right at the heart of the interview he states, 'It's at times of stress when you don't read the Bible but the Bible reads you and that [sic] sometimes it doesn't need too much interpretative sauce.'[9] He is saying something hugely important here, which not only gives a hermeneutical key to unlock how he himself understands his own interpretative strategy, how he is actually using the Bible in this interview, but also sheds light on the process of the way many Christians use the Bible all the time, including John Ruskin

Fraser is claiming several things, the truth of which can be observed in the body of the interview itself. First he is giving testimony that at this time of stress both the deep values and the actual words of the Bible come to him and 'read him', by which he would seem to indicate that they open him up to seeing and understanding what he most deeply believes and cares about, that they challenge him to act, that they create the framework for his responses and perhaps that they in some sense sit in critical judgment on the whole situation, his own part included. This is an extremely powerful claim.

It is, as in the case of Ruskin, made by a man who knows his Bible, specifically the Gospels, as the evidence of the interview shows. Furthermore his claim of not needing much interpretative sauce is slightly disingenuous. While he means prima facie that there is a plain sense of the Bible message in this case which doesn't bear petty equivocation, he is himself actually speaking from a place in which he is the heir to a substantial interpretative tradition – the interpretative sauce has been

---

[9] For this, and all other quotations in this part relating to the interview, see Rusbridger, 'A Troublesome Priest?'.

well digested and absorbed into his system. However, it is entirely true that he is himself in this moment caught up in a 'gut reaction' in which there is identification with the gospel text but no self-reflective critical distance.

There are in fact at least two major traditions out of which Fraser is speaking in this interview, and indeed out of which he is acting, so his identification is not 'unmediated'. These are not only traditions of interpretation but traditions of practice. The first is the Anglican tradition of incarnational theology. He talks several times of the incarnation, of a 'raw, incarnational, practical faith' which 'can't be indifferent to the physical circumstances under which people live'. This is not only to indwell a broad Anglican tradition but also a specific Anglo-Catholic tradition of 'slum-priests'; of life and ministry in the inner city; of the service of God with us in the poor as the other side of the service of God with us in the Sacrament. It was to St Paul's Bethnal Green in the East End of London that he went when St Paul's Cathedral was closed because of the protest, 'It was catholic, inner city worship and for me it caught a particular aspect of what I believe, which is, as it were, more "incarnation" than Wren ever tried to do.'

The second tradition of interpretation and practice out of which Fraser speaks and acts is liberation theology. This is not explicitly named and may be a more general influence, but its voice can be heard in such expressions as 'Jesus born in a stable, the sort of church that exists for the poor and marginalised.' Likewise the sermon on Matthew's 'render unto Caesar', which he recalls preaching on the first Sunday of the protest, connects that passage to Matthew chapter 6 and the Sermon on the Mount, to not serving God and money, a specifically liberationist interpretation which says as Fraser does in the article, 'you can't just say "let money, let the state, let all those issues stay on one side and let you do your piety on another"'. The Anglo-Catholic tradition of incarnational theology and solidarity with the poor is coupled with a liberationist theology of option for the poor and political and social-structural critique. The particular reading that the Bible makes of Giles Fraser in a time of stress is as it would be for all of us – it is the reading that we already own and practice in our hearts and lives.

When we observe what Fraser actually draws from the Bible we see that his theological understanding of his own actions and of appropriate Christian response and practice derive substantially from Jesus Christ. While he does refer once to St Paul's practice as a tent maker and once to the whole Bible – 'Money is the number one moral issue in the Bible' – most of the time he goes direct to Jesus. He does this in three ways.

First, there is the appeal to the incarnation as the foundation of Christian involvement in the world. Christianity is a religion that cares for human beings and for their material living conditions because the Christian God became human flesh and lived on this earth: 'As Christians you are called to engage with the world: that's the whole nature of the Incarnation.'

Second, there is a move almost like a sophisticated version of 'what would Jesus do?'. It comes out in views that run from 'Jesus wants to point us to a bigger picture of the world than simply shopping', which could be said to be just a contextualised version of Jesus' words to us in the Gospels, through to 'saying he thinks Jesus would be more extreme than him on the shape of modern capitalism' or a reference to '"centrist views" of the sort Jesus would have found unremarkable'. In Fraser's account this is a way of translating Jesus' teachings into a modern context – see again 'markets were made for man and not man for market' – but it is a method that holds within itself an understanding: that what Jesus might think (does think?) of the present situation is relevant for Christians. This implies both a robust doctrine of the ongoing work of the God in the world which is continuous with God's working in Christ and, connected with this, a direct contemporary relevance and translatability of the Bible into contemporary issues. This is Fraser's version of 'Our priests don't even warn our Chancellor of the Exchequer of such unlawfulness', and of Spencer's superimposition of Christ entering Jerusalem onto Cookham High Street.[10]

Third, Fraser quotes the Bible directly, though he mixes the actual words of 1 Timothy with Jesus' teaching: 'Jesus is very clear that the love of money is the root of all evil.' Interestingly he does such direct referencing of the Bible very little. Also interesting is what he does (and doesn't do) with this teaching of Jesus'. He uses it in the context of answering a question about the protest on his doorstep. He does not condemn capitalism, saying he used to be a socialist but is one no longer. He criticises wealth creation for the few, saying that both anger and anxiety about this is legitimate. The implication is general but not necessarily the less powerful; Jesus' words are harnessed to endorse an attack at the way current wealth creation and distribution bring inequalities and hardship to the human community. The preoccupation here is with the flourishing of human community – a preoccupation that Ruskin shared, and to which both Ruskin and Fraser would insist that Jesus was centrally committed.

Personal and Public

This text is both personal and public, as was the action it explores. It displays the drama of a man walking out of 'England's most majestic cathedral'. The text opens and closes with what he is wearing – from 'black jeans, T-shirt and stubble' to 'he borrows an electric razor and a white shirt ... strips to the waist ... pulls on his jacket.' We know where he lives – and is about to leave – 'a 17th-century grace and favour house in the shadow of Wren's cathedral'; and we hear of the personal anxiety about the step he has taken: 'I have a family and kids. I am terrified. I mean I have no other job to go to.' The interview directly addresses the motivations and views of an individual man in the midst of a crisis public enough to warrant front and central pages of national daily newspapers.

This public debate was catapulted into the national consciousness, not only by the fact that Occupy London Stock Exchange chose to camp outside St Paul's, but by the actions of the St Paul's authorities in initially being willing to cooperate

---

[10] See Chapter 5.

with the Corporation of London in asking the police to remove the camp, and by Fraser's consequent resignation. It became very quickly a debate in which the church's actions were subject to scrutiny as much as the state's – indeed the protesters complained that all attention had been turned on the church. Unlike the Kairos Palestine document which we will look at in the next chapter (but similarly to the South African Kairos document which inspired it) the church is set up for criticism as much as the state here. Fraser's reference to Wat Tyler, picked up in the *Guardian* headline, is significant; Tyler was the leader of the Peasant's Revolt in 1381. They marched on the city of London and killed the Archbishop of Canterbury.

Performed and Performative

In this case, these private and public factors shade into our next characteristic of a text of reflective public theology – that it is both performed and performative. This is clearly the case here in a straightforward sense. Fraser had already performed his text: he resigned. That is why he was in the newspaper. This text and others like it are clearly also performative – not only did Fraser's action precipitate movement and change in the decisions made, and acted on, at St Paul's and elsewhere in respect of the Occupy London camp, but his reported action brought huge response in the media and from ordinary citizens, including many church people. His action changed things; and so did the texts that addressed it, including our text in which he begins some reflection, albeit raw 'reflection-in-action'.

It should be noted, however, that the reason Fraser resigned, his 'red line', as he puts it, 'was about using violence in the name of the church to move people on … I feel that the church cannot answer peaceful protest with violence.' This is interesting, because the whole 'theological reflection' of the interview is about wealth and the Bible. But the actual trigger for action, which set up the interview in the first place, was about peace and violence. Fraser had already set out his public stall on wealth, as head of the St Paul's Institute he was committed to open public discussion of issues of wealth and money and communal well-being, but chose to do this from a location in the Established Church, within the cathedral of Christopher Wren – 'Wren's forte was not Jesus born in a stable' – and in the heart of the City. What we find here is not careful, systematic, theological reflection. At this point in the process Fraser is giving us what is closest to his heart, a refusal to condone the threatened violence, which ultimately led to his resignation. Although it was not any critique of wealth creation that made Fraser resign, the 'seeing with the heart' is laced with incarnational and liberation theology while working within and from an institution of power and influence in the Established Church.

Carefully and Creatively Crafted

The text we read about Fraser was carefully and creatively crafted, not by Giles Fraser but by Alan Rusbridger. The text, proclaimed as an exclusive interview, involves the selection of a headline and bold quotations and a very large photograph of a serious and thoughtful Fraser, shaven and wearing a white shirt and jacket. Is this a text of *The Guardian* or a text of Giles Fraser? It is both. It is Fraser mediated by another context, a different but overlapping set of interests. While the case of a newspaper interview makes this point starkly it is none the less true of many texts of public theology, not least of the Gospels, that a 'voice' is heard mediated by other 'evangelists'.

The process of careful crafting is shaped by interests; in turn the crafted product shapes the responses of the reader. The expert rendering of an interview, written up with all the artifice and rhetorical devices of a professional journalist, presents the material in a deliberate way and engages the reader. My own reading of Fraser's actions and words have been shaped by what Rusbridger decided to tell and show; Rusbridger has controlled the impact – for example in highlighting the opulence of the church and in foregrounding the strength of Jesus' message about money. The interview form displays starkly the selection and interpretation that is in fact part of all so-called 'descriptive' rendering of an object, person or situation.[11] Furthermore, careful rhetorical crafting is an essential ingredient of making a text attractive and engaging to readers in the public domain, and thus of gaining a public at all.

Some Final Reflections

In analysing this newspaper interview I have taken what I earlier called the third or reflective text, the first two being the text of the Bible and the text of life. This reflective moment, I argued, is followed by the text of performance and action. In Rusbridger's interview with Fraser that fourth text is determinative; it is probably only because Fraser resigned that the interview happened at all. Reflection and action are here therefore inextricably intertwined. Even the giving of the interview was a deliberate part of the performance and action. Reflection and action are not always so demonstrably conjoined, but I offer this as a limit situation which displays a crucial element present in all true theological reflection but which is not always so blatantly clear.

It was a sentence about the Bible that drew me to this interview in the first instance, and it is the analysis of Fraser's natural and unembarrassed use of the Bible in this very public, non-ecclesial, human and controversial context that most interests me. 'It's at times of stress when you don't read the Bible but the Bible reads you.' At first sight it may seem that I have rather betrayed my 'reader' orientation (Chapter 1) in being so drawn to this experience Fraser describes. On the contrary, the emphasis is firmly on the reader, but the extremity of the human situation means that Fraser is thrown back on what is in his heart and mind, to what is *in* him, to what he has learned in his community and internalised in his soul. And the Bible speaks to him from his own depths. He does not so much

---

11   See Chapter 6.

'make' connections in an analytical way as 'see' connections, as he looks at what is around him and what is happening to him. In this he is deeply Ruskinian.

Chapter 10
A Crisis and a Judgement Call:
The Bible and International Conflict

The crisis in the Middle East has been a central issue of international relations in recent times, and close to the heart of this agony is the situation in Israel/Palestine. Even to name the place and its historical events is to enter the conflict. Since, and indeed even before, the creation of the State of Israel in 1948, there has been dispute over the right to live in and on this land. The year 1948 is variously remembered as a cause of rejoicing, the 'War of Liberation', or as a cause of mourning, the 'Nakba' or catastrophe. This issue was further exacerbated in 1967 with the annexation of East Jerusalem, the West Bank and Gaza. Fear and pain caused by actions on both sides of the conflict, and crucially also by the powerful agendas, policies and actions, both open and hidden, of international actors in the drama, not only poison this 'Holy Land' of three religions, but also are one root of the unresolvable tensions and wars in the Middle East and beyond that in the global arena.

I have chosen a text from this context not only because this issue is of inestimable significance in the international public sphere, but because it embeds within it as one factor in its complexity a dispute over the Bible's use. Furthermore this dispute not only has an intra-Christian dimension but an intra-Jewish dimension and a Jewish-Christian dimension. The text I have chosen is a specifically Christian one, though it addresses Jews and Muslims too. At the heart of it lies a question about the promises in the Bible concerning the land, and about Christian interpretation of these in the light of a wider question about a Christian understanding of God's promises to the Jews and what role these play in a Christian reading of God's purposes for the world. The Bible thus is a central and a disputed text for this document as it has been throughout the history of the Church, as is manifested by attitudes to the Jews and the Hebrew Bible. The Bible itself, and the contested use made of it by different faith communities, becomes a public issue.

The Kairos Palestine Document – December 2009

The Kairos Palestine document was produced by leaders in the Palestinian Christian community and endorsed by the heads of a wide and comprehensive group of churches, denoting themselves as 'the Patriarchs and Heads of Churches in Jerusalem'.[1] Those who produced it are Palestinian Christians, prominent leaders in the community – writers, academics, public speakers, leaders of organisations and community activists, many with an international profile. The document, they say, 'is not a theoretical theological study or a policy paper, but is rather a document of faith and work', arising from a year's study in prayer, discussion and consultation. It is offered as an expression of the views and concerns of the Palestinian people. Its political context is not only the wider question of Israel and Palestine, but the specific process which unfolded after 2000, known as the Second or 'Al-Aqsa' Intifada, and since 2001 the post 9/11 international 'war on terror'. Its theological context includes the movement known as Palestinian Liberation Theology, as represented particularly in the presence on the writing group of Dr Naim Ateek, a founder of Sabeel, the Ecumenical Liberation Theology Center in Jerusalem.

The document seeks to be prophetic, defining this as 'addressing things as they are without equivocation' and having boldness. It is specific in what it condemns – the mechanisms of Israeli oppression and what it names as 'apartheid' – in what it calls for – the establishment of an independent state with Al-Quds – Jerusalem – as its capital – and in its demands of its readers – international pressure on Israel including legal measures to end oppression and disregard for international law, and non-violent resistance by all Palestinians.

'A word of faith, hope, and love from the heart of Palestinian suffering' is the subtitle of the document, indicating that it springs from and is contextually located in human experience. It is theology spoken from suffering and from the heart. Despite its disclaimer that it is not 'a theoretical theological paper' it is clearly intentionally 'theological' in the sense that it is reflection arising from faith, it deploys the language of faith from the beginning – a 'word to the world', 'we wanted to see the Glory of the grace of God in this land' – and it makes a specific connection to an existing Christian document of public theology from the South African struggle against apartheid, the 'Kairos document' published in 1985. Furthermore the document uses the Bible extensively and critically to make its points.

Something which immediately strikes the reader who is already familiar with the South African Kairos document, is that this new 'kairos document' comes with the blessing of the church and its leaders, whereas its predecessor came with a critique of 'church theology' alongside its critique of 'state theology'. The writers of the South African Kairos document had to wrestle with the problem of the church in South Africa. Here the church in a Palestinian context is seen and named as onside, indeed the document comes with an express endorsement from the highest echelons of key church communities in the region.

The text is certainly carefully crafted and designed to be performative. It is both personal and public, and it is without doubt rooted in the contemporary

---

[1]	The full document, a list of Palestinian Christian institutions and personalities who signed it and more information can be found at http://www.kairospalestine.ps/sites/default/ Documents/English.pdf (accessed 02.11.11).

situation and draws on the Christian heritage. In this it is a classic 'third text' of theological reflection. There are, however, some immediately apparent contrasts with the text examined in the last chapter. This is an officially published document of a group of churches – an ecumenical statement deliberately designed to do work in the public arena by persuasion. It arose from a long process of deliberation and was launched on a website in the context of intentional promotion as in itself a theological intervention in a publicly contested issue. It makes the Bible an important focus of its reflection and as well as *using* it within its argument, also argues for a specific interpretation.

There is a form of church theology being critiqued here, and it is the Zionist theology of many churches in the world. The word Zionist is carefully not used but the target of the critique is clear – 'Furthermore we know that certain theologians in the West try to attach a biblical and theological legitimacy to the infringement of our rights' (2.3.3). In so doing, the document claims, such theologians make the promises (of God in the Bible) 'a menace to our very existence' and the '"good news"' a '"harbinger of death"'. A certain sort of church theology is problematised but one that is seen as belonging to foreigners, 'the West', not to the Christian context in which the document arises. Thus it is not in the same way a contextual internal critique, though it *is* an internal Christian critique at the macro level.

It is important to note this matter in particular at the outset as it plunges the reader directly into a controversy concerning how the Bible should be read, one that goes to the centre of the Bible's interpretation: how should the 'Old' and 'New' Testaments be read in relation to each other, and what is the heart of future expectation of the delivery of God's promises to humanity? This is no idle question and has an immediate context and location in which it is played out in a very this worldly and political way – the right to possession of a particular piece of land. That is the context in which this document sets it, with a subsection headed 'Our land has a universal mission' (2.3–2.5). Lurking behind the discussion at this point in the document are two opposite Christian perspectives in respect of understanding Jewish existence today: the perspective that sees the return of the Jews to the land of Israel as part of the outworking of God's promises (characterised often in public debate as 'Zionist') and the perspective that sees God's promises to the Jews not literally to be fulfilled in return to the land but spiritually in the reconciliation of all humanity, Jews included, to God in Christ (characterised often in public debate as 'supersessionist'). We shall need to return to this debate as we look in detail at how the Kairos Palestine document uses the Bible.

How does the Kairos Palestine Document use the Bible?

The first thing to be said is that this document is peppered with quotations from the Bible, both Hebrew Scriptures/Old Testament and New Testament. Where the Bible is not directly quoted the text is full of allusive biblical words and phrases. Furthermore its whole conceptualisation, as a 'word to' takes the reader straight into a biblical/prophetic idea and practice – God's timely word spoken to challenge the hearers.

This 'word' of God in the Bible is quite specifically appropriated. Its target audience is named, interestingly in the final sections: our Christian brothers and sisters, the Churches of the world, the international community, Jewish and Muslim religious leaders, our Palestinian people and the Israeli people. In each case, and throughout the document, there is a very precise rooting in the political, social and economic realities of contemporary Palestinian existence.

The appeal to scripture is, however, quite general for the most part. The document seeks to centre its ethical and religious values in the Bible, taking faith, hope and love (1 Cor. 13) as structuring concepts/practices and deploying biblical quotations either to reinforce argument as it goes along or actually to head up sections – for example, section 3 on 'hope' is headed up with a quotation from Romans 8: 'If God is for us, who is against us?' A striking example of this is section 4, which concerns love, and in particular how love might be shown at the same time as and in the context of resistance to a named evil and injustice. This is an extremely delicate matter, for Palestinians, for Israeli Jews and for the international community, all addressees of the document. The section is headed up by no less than four direct quotations from the New Testament, two from the Gospels and two from the Letters, giving the impression to the reader of an attempt to assert the authority of scripture to reinforce a point. Immediately after the quotations, leading off the discussion, is the short but firm sentence: 'This word is clear.'

God's word in itself is, in this document, considered to be quite clear. It is not considered problematic, any more than the church is. It is taken to be clear in its meaning, and life-giving in its effects. 'The word of God is a word of love for all His creation' (6.1). There are certain principles underlying the use of the Bible here – a proclaimed trust in a 'plain meaning' of the text, a presumed strong identification of 'God's word' with the Bible, a universal thrust for this word, a Christological interpretation, an assumption that it is good news for all and an identification of this with certain values – faith, hope and the logic of love (5.4.2), and also peace and justice and the dignity of all people created by God.

There are certain places where a more specific reading of the Bible is made, and in one of these the idea is introduced that in practice at least its effects may not be altogether benign. It concerns the fact that in history the Bible has been used to legitimate a wide variety of practices and in particular all kinds of political regimes. At section 3.4 the document, in addressing 'the mission of the Church', speaks of proclaiming the Kingdom of God (3.4.2). This kingdom of God is identified with certain values – justice, peace and human dignity – and a biblical quotation is used to assert its presence in human society, on earth not just in heaven – Luke 17.21 'The Kingdom of God is among you' (3.4.4). This thrust of identifying the Kingdom of God with values lived out on earth, however, shies away from identifying the Kingdom of God with any particular earthly 'kingdom', quoting John 18.36 'my kingdom is not from this world', and

Romans 14.17 'the Kingdom of God is not food and drink but righteousness and peace and joy in the Holy Spirit', to make the point that the Kingdom of God stands always in opposition to the legitimising of unjust political regimes and the violation of human dignity (3.4.3).

Section 2 of the document is where the question of how we understand the Bible is explicitly introduced, and where the struggle over different interpretations is directly named. This struggle appears quite clearly in this document as a rejection of the 'fundamentalist Biblical interpretation' (2.2.2) of 'certain theologians in the West' (2.3.3) which is used 'as a weapon in our present history' (2.2.2) to legitimise infringement of Palestinian Christian rights (2.3.3), thus making the gospel to them, a menace and a '"harbinger of death"'.

Here the possibility that the Bible might be neither clear nor life-giving is raised. It is not *clear* because generations have struggled over a Christian understanding of the place of Jews in the plans of God, and what are nowadays named respectively as Zionist and supersessionist models of understanding this (though never so named in this document) have very different perspectives on the land of Israel/Palestine and the God-given rights of Jews and others to live there.[2] Neither is the Bible always *life-giving* because the assertion of Jewish right to the land – rooted as it is in the biblical text based on the promise to Abraham, Isaac and Jacob, renewed at the Burning Bush in Exodus 3 and including not only the story of a people liberated from slavery but the story of their driving out the indigenous inhabitants – has in practice legitimated injustice to Palestinians, just as, though it is not said here, the assertion of the supersession of Judaism by Christianity, justified from the New Testament texts such as Galatians 6.16 and the Epistle to the Hebrews, has legitimated centuries of Christian persecution of Jews.

The principles accepted in this document of understanding the relationship between the Hebrew Scriptures and the Christian New Testament are here clearly expounded. Theologically a Trinitarian creedal statement is set first in the overall section (2.1), thus the biblical interpretation is guided by a set of beliefs in God as loving creator, in Christ as saviour of the world and in the Holy Spirit who helps us to understand the revelation of God in scripture. *The reading of the Old and New Testaments as a unity is set within this creedal statement.* In practice this unity is the result of a Christological imposition, as is made immediately clear by the quotation from Hebrew 1.1–2 at the head of the next section 'How do we understand the word of God?' 'Long ago God spoke ... by the prophets, but in these last days God has spoken to us by a Son' (2.2). This interpretation relies on the periodisation of history, the contrast between letters of stone and the living spirit, and a universalising of 'the promises, the election, the people of God and the

2   For contrasting views, see W.D. Davies, *The Gospel and the Land: Early Christianity and Jewish Territorial Doctrine* (Sheffield: JSOT Press, 1994); Nur Masalha, *The Bible and Zionism: Invented Traditions, Archaeology and Post-Colonialism in Israel-Palestine* (London and New York: Zed Books, 2007); Rosemary Radford Ruether, *Faith and Fratricide: The Theological Roots of Anti-Semitism* (Eugene, Ore.: Wipf and Stock, 1974).

land' (2.2.2). The promise to Abraham, therefore, becomes a promise to all people, as Galatians 3 indicates.

While this document unashamedly espouses a particular Christological interpretation, it does not hide the fact that there are competing interpretations, and it makes an attempt to engage with these, or at least to deny them. While it may look at first as if that denial is based on assertion rather than careful and detailed argument, it is in fact based on two fundamental factors of great importance. First it is based in a founding belief about the character of God as universally just and loving, and second it is based in the reality of contemporary human suffering – 'It is a matter of life and death' (2.3.4). Observing that there is a causal connection between certain theology and that suffering, the writers of the document declare that God may not be 'subordinate[d] ... to temporary human interests' (2.5), and that the transforming of religion into human ideology 'strip[s] the Word of God of its holiness, it universality and its truth' (2.4). The underlying assumptions are that the Bible unequivocally presents a God of goodness and justice, and that where the Bible is used to bring death this must stem from a misinterpretation. The prioritisation of certain themes, as constituting the essence of the Bible's message, is crucial for this approach. That there is a problem with how the Bible is interpreted is signalled by a current practice of injustice.

It is important to struggle with the Bible in this way, and many Christians would agree with the writers of this document that the struggle is only over the interpretation, and the problem is with the readers and their distortions and misuse. But others would go further, and would see that the struggle and the problem are within the biblical text itself. Is it the case that the God-warranted treatment of the Canaanites and the patriarchal promises in the Hebrew Scriptures on the one hand, and the anti-Jewish material in the New Testament on the other, have in themselves, and not just in inappropriate interpretation and distorted use, fed and legitimated respectively the injustices and cruelty perpetrated on Palestinians and on Jews?

A central contention of the Kairos Palestine document is that God's love, justice and good favour are universal towards all peoples and that using the Bible to support and legitimate 'political options and positions that are based upon injustice' or oppression of one group by another is wrong (2.4). This is described as transforming religion into human ideology, and is rejected. Again this only goes part of the way to addressing a problem of the use of the Bible in public theology. It is a crucially important part of the way – the rejection of uses of the Bible that bring death in the name of God – but we need to dig deeper into this issue. *All* use of the Bible is in one sense ideological, not just *some* uses, and this needs to be recognised, because as Gadamer pointed out, all of us as interpreters have our biblical interpretations formed by the culture of which we are a part. There is not some universal position of general godly benevolence, unrelated to specific human conditions and contexts, from which we can interpret. The moment that we begin to act and talk in the real world we have to contextualise, we inevitably see partially – partially in the sense of only in part and partially in the sense of with a vested interest. That is true of every position of biblical interpretation.

In summary, the Kairos Palestine document offers us an example of the use of the Bible in public theology that is born of passion – in human suffering and a deep sense of injustice. It speaks with boldness of both contemporary reality and the Christian tradition, drawing explicitly and repeatedly on the biblical text. It is carefully crafted to do its work in a targeted public realm, and while calling for action its very publication is in itself a performance of witness. It is debatable whether it offers, or intends indeed to offer, any new interpretation, and it falls short of a deeper level of questioning that wrestles with the problems of its own arguments as well as those of others. It does not address the inherent problems within the biblical text itself. As a result it states with passion some very important aspects of theology and faith which have bearing on the contemporary agonies, but that agony never enters the theology and faith itself in the document. This may blunt its effects, as the presence of those agonies *within* the Christian tradition itself often hold back the Christian community from the levels of international support that the writers of the document seek (7). To assume that the logic of love and not the 'logic of force' (7) is of the essence of the biblical and Christian tradition and can be simply appealed to and easily identified in practice is to beg the crucial question.

***

Giles Fraser offered us an example of a person under pressure, grasping the fundamental biblical shaping of his own life. In the interview with him we see reflection *in* action rather than reflection *on* action. This is reflection on the hoof, in the midst of action, raw and incomplete, as our reflection always is, refracted by the perspective of the interviewer who chooses what he wants to include and to emphasise. It draws on reflections of the past and acknowledges the instinctive and the impulsive – 'in moments of stress you don't read the Bible, the Bible reads you'. The placards of the protestors in the street mirrored back to him the very biblical texts that were in his heart.

The Kairos Palestine document offers an example of a public use of the Bible driven by human need and human passion. It indicates a rather different kind of reflectiveness. While born out of action and conflict it takes a longer term stance on a specific contested area of biblical interpretation: the election, the land of Israel and the promises to the Jewish people, and the link with a specific historical/ contemporary people, the state of Israel. It rejects this link, on the grounds that it brings death to Palestinians, and legitimates actions that contradict the major theme of justice and peace for all which, it suggests, pervades the Bible, notwithstanding ancient promises of the land to Israel and the threat of dispossession of the indigenous populations. Its criticism and reflectiveness, however, does not go further and ask questions of what the other view also found in the Bible, the account that sees the election, the land and the promises fulfilled and superseded in Christianity, has legitimated by way of bringing death to the Jewish people over the years. There is enthusiasm for the Bible, but ambivalence about the Bible is not fully recognised in the interpretation offered.

In our examination of John Ruskin in Part II we found a similar passion able to 'make strange' and ask questions of the world in which he lived, based on the response of the heart and the prophetic spirit to injustices in the world around him. However, we need to be frank about the fact that he, like the authors of the Kairos Palestine document and like Giles Fraser, was a man of his time. He was not always able to detach himself from the old-fashioned Tory world in which he had been raised and in which he lived and which he admitted he naturally fitted. His critique of capitalism is based on a gut reaction and a reading of the Bible that runs: 'the Bible is against the accumulation of wealth which means oppression of the poor, and is in favour of life; but I see the opposite going on everywhere in a supposedly Christian society'. A vital message for any theologian, however, practical or otherwise, is that any 'self-interest' – including one's own and that of the poor – should be held up to scrutiny and should be itself the subject of self-examination, preferably by themselves and not by their opponents. If this is not done there is a hermeneutical deficit, and we may be embracing that which we find congenial in the Bible while not allowing its strangeness and awkwardness to challenge our viewpoint. As Paul Ballard writes, 'This kind of wisdom comes only from letting the Bible, *in all its diversity and strangeness*, become a companion along the way': companion, yes, but a strange one and one that may bring contradiction and diversity of perspective.[3]

---

[3] Ballard, 'The Use of Scripture', p. 169; my italics.

Chapter 11
Towards a Biblically Informed Practical and Public Theology

As I write this, I am sitting in Wesley House Dining Room, surrounded by six of my professional doctorate candidates and colleagues. It is a writing day, so there is absolute silence except for the wind soughing wildly in the trees outside the upper windows.

People keep coming and going to Annual Monitoring Reviews, Confirmation of Candidature, the library, an educational consultant. Some are almost ready to submit, some just embarking on Stage 2 theses. Bit by bit they are getting there, slowly, painfully up the mountain of doctoral research, constantly overtaken, never daring to look at how far there is to go, or how difficult it is. They are doing things that will change their bit of the world as a result of the reflection on their practice – education of Black boys, a free school, the self-respect of unpaid workers, Catholic family ministry, Anglican local church leadership, research in the Church of England, CAFOD, the YMCA. They are doing things that will change them personally forever. Knowledge produced through critical interrogation of one's own context and tradition is hard won.

Since 2006 I have been involved, along with colleagues in my own and other universities, in running a Professional Doctorate in Practical Theology. For those of us involved it has been one of the most exciting adventures of our professional lives. We have seen unfolding before us what it means to put practice in the driving seat of advanced academic work and research. The centre and core of the idea of a professional doctorate is that the research starts in practice, one's *own* practice, moves to theory and returns to practice. What appears to be a superficially simple move has the profoundest consequences. First, it means the recognition that all the research starts from a particular context, and from specific practice within that context. The emergence of the research question is problem-based and action-driven; it is local and focused. Second, it means that all the research relates to the practice of the researcher, and self-reflexivity is, therefore, a key component. Investigating and analysing one's own environment, practices and reactions is of the essence of the work. Finally, this way of doing practical theology locates the discipline in a new context; theology becomes a partner not only of history, philosophy and ancient languages, or even of sociology and the human sciences, but also of other practice-related disciplines such as music therapy, education and health and social care.

> Let those who teach theology in seminaries and universities strive to collaborate with men versed in the other sciences through a sharing of their resources and points of view. Theological inquiry should pursue a profound understanding of revealed truth; at the same time it should not neglect close contact with its own time that it may be able to help these men [sic] skilled in various disciplines to attain to a better understanding of the faith.[1]

This practice of practical theology is therefore unremittingly located in the contemporary world; it is by its very nature public theology. It indeed shares its form of enquiry with other practice-based research disciplines in the university, and its mode of textual production is shaped by the need to demonstrate certain 'doctoral' qualities (the contribution to knowledge and the knowledge of the wider area of study within which the subject matter of the thesis is located) in the researcher to the examiners; however, that is by no means the only context in which this work finds a public audience. Much of this research is published in journals or books, which have a professional practitioner audience as well as an academic one, and, most significantly, the work people do on this programme feeds into their working contexts with the aim of transforming them. This may sometimes be a process that meets with resistance as much as welcome, as taken-for-granted ways of understanding and doing things are exposed and challenged.

An expression has kept recurring to me as I have been writing this book: 'in the cracks'. This is no accident. The critical negotiation of our own history and practices which I am advocating as a basis for using the Bible in practical and public theology must happen *in medias res*, in the midst of life. Cracks in a pavement, a wall or crevices for hand-holds on a rock face are an evocative image of this.

The Professional Doctorate has lived 'in the cracks' of its own context. It has grown in a crack – on the margins – of Anglia Ruskin University, a secular university with Ruskin's name, which has apparently little time for Ruskin and no place for Theology, except in the Cambridge Theological Federation, its marginal, partner

---

[1]   http://www.vatican.va/archive/hist_councils/ii_vatican_council/documents/vat-ii_const_19651207_gaudium-et-spes_en.html (accessed 31.07.12); see Zoë Bennett and Elaine Graham, 'The Professional Doctorate in Practical Theology: Developing the Researching Professional in Practical Theology in Higher Education', *Journal of Adult Theological Education*, 5.1 (2008): 33–51; and further, Zoë Bennett, 'Evaluating the Feasibility of a Cross-Institutional Professional Doctorate in Practical Theology: Project Report', *Discourse*, 6.2 (2007): 55–77; Elaine L. Graham, 'The Professional Doctorate in Practical Theology: An Idea Whose Time has Come?', *International Journal of Practical Theology*, 10.2 (March 2007): 298–311; Zoë Bennett, 'Theology and the Researching Professional: The Professional Doctorate in Practical Theology', *Theology*, CXII.869 (2009): 333–43.

institution. But this secular context is key to what the Professional Doctorate is all about; it is in the world, secular. *It has grown in a crack in the Cambridge Theological Federation too – in a group of institutions where ordination training dominates, where research fights for time and priority, and where running something from the centre for external students is an exception to the norm of residential training. It has grown in a crack in 'Cambridge': this work is not being done in the distinguished Faculty of Divinity in the University of Cambridge, where such 'vocational' and practical theology is not a priority, for its subject matter has not flourished in an academic world of 'theory and texts first', or of models and methodologies, or in the safety of respectability through form and through imitation and precedent.*

I too live in the cracks. My writing, which is done in the tiny cracks between the interruptions of interviews and encounters with the students, is fructified by reflection on so many things that happen in the various encounters that superficially seem to get in the way. Such self-involvement may distract and distort, if not reflected on, but it may fructify and shape intellectual life if reflected on. So it is with these supposed interruptions – the struggling back to the heart of what makes one student tick, the listening to the painful emotions of another, hearing another use his voice. My solo voice is deeply embedded in this choir and my process is their process as theirs is mine. BUT within these cracks fragile wallflowers of all sorts can grow. All the people sitting in this room with me bring the world in with them: 'The blizzard, the blizzard of the world has crossed the threshold, and it's overcome the borders of the soul.'[2]

Why do I do this? Why has it become the project of my professional life? I ask this because it is the question I would ask of any of my students on the doctorate. Why do you do this? What is driving you? What do you most care about? I am a teacher and a naturally intellectually curious person. And I believe that God is to be found in human beings, who are the most precious things in the world. And so engagement with them is the *way of learning and this way of understanding is crucial to me. This learner-centred pedagogy shows that knowledge may be produced through a complex process of self-reflection: looking in enables good looking out; and the thing we can most properly know is ourselves, but in knowing ourselves we can know so much else. It also gives people voice. Changing things is important too: changing things in the world. The Professional Doctorate is about actually doing things. But it is about doing things in the context of that radical self-reflexivity that enables criticality. And so it is about having the courage to see contradictions. In the midst of it all it is coming to terms with ourselves, and with our own painful emotions and contradictions. This penetration deeper and deeper is what practical theology and the Professional Doctorate are all about. That is why I am willing to expend so much on it – so much of my intuitive self and so much of my analytical self.*

---

[2]   Leonard Cohen, 'The Future', in *Stranger Music: Selected Poems and Songs* (London: Jonathan Cape, 1993), p. 370. Copyright © 1993 Leonard Cohen. Reprinted by permission of McClelland & Stewart

Ruskin, in his inaugural lecture for the Cambridge School of Art, talked about sight being the most important thing – not light but sight. Religion talks a lot about light, but without sight it is not effective. The seeing, insightful, human being is at the heart of knowledge and at the heart of living. The acting, knowing, seeing subject is also the loving subject. Human emotions and aesthetic sensitivities are at the heart of knowledge and of life. This is connected to the Ruskin who is ambivalent, loving, hating, wrestling with, delicately balanced towards the Bible – unable to get free from it but in later life able to criticise it with both playfulness and distance, but also with incredible closeness, bound in a dialectical relationship. Ruskin is the acting, knowing, seeing, wrestling subject. But, at times, it is so, so fragile, so precarious, as can be seen in Rose's death and in the madness of Ruskin's later years. I value and love in Ruskin an incredible strength found in places of great weakness – the fragility of human knowing, and its robustness.

As I have been writing this book, I have found myself going round and round, to 'know the place for the first time, '[3] doing what I get my students to do – that is to keep going back and back into what is the well spring of what they are doing, and to see how it shapes and drives their research question, possibly at times warps it, but when recognised, can elucidate its truth and display its beauty. My key question is 'How can we use the Bible with love and tenderness, with playful imagination, with a criticality that does not destroy it but elucidates its truth and displays its beauty?' But why do I want to use it that way? It is because if I do I am not caught in that place where I was caught all those years ago when I thought I would go mad if I didn't solve the inerrancy/infallibility issue. Tenderness, love, playfulness, imagination and a critical awareness that can keep some reserve and a distance but can still elucidate the truth and display the beauty of the other are crucial. If I live with these, I will be able to live well, or at least well enough. It is about both warmth and ambivalence to the Christian tradition and to the Bible. It is about an entirely unsystematic approach to making connections between the world and the Bible. In fact it's not about making them at all; it's about seeing *them.*

I began this book autobiographically, and I have ended it autobiographically. Reflection on the Professional Doctorate programme provides a personal 'text' or testimonial for examining how the Bible may be used in public and practical theology. The practice of the Professional Doctorate itself is inextricably linked with the central theses of this book. That is to say, the practices of using the Bible in public theology, which are explored and advocated in this book through an engagement with John Ruskin, are the same practices that are embedded in the processes of the Professional Doctorate. The categories of engagement between the book of the Bible and the book of life that emerge from disciplined attention to the practices of the Professional Doctorate resonate with the characteristics of

---

3   T.S. Eliot, 'Little Gidding' from *Four Quartets*, in *Collected Poems 1909–1962* (London: Faber and Faber, 1963), p. 222. Reprinted by permission of Faber and Faber Ltd.

biblical interpretation discovered in Ruskin's life and work. Through this double focus the key practices of using the Bible in public and practical theology, which constitute the heart of this book, begin to take a final form: as follows.

The Importance of Context

I begin with context. That is both literally the case – I have just written about the Professional Doctorate while sitting in a room next door to my own office surrounded by students and staff on the programme – and also conceptually so – if I want to conceptualise the method of practical and public theology characteristic of the Professional Doctorate, including the use of the Bible, I start with the people and with what they actually do. 'What they actually do' has two references. It refers to the living and working context that each member of the programme brings into it and researches. Second, it refers to how they do practical theology, and specifically here to how they use the Bible. Candidates come in with dispositions, histories, practices, commitments, hopes and fears – and confusions – in respect of the Bible. Each has a different starting place, different priorities, a different way of seeing; each has a different set of moves whereby they do or do not 'see' or 'make' connections between the text of the Bible and the text of life. Our aim on the programme is not to give a set way of 'using the Bible in public theology' but to enable critical reflexivity on the actualities and particulars of all of these things for each person.

Working with Ruskin has enabled a very different historical context in which to offer a fresh perspective on my own context and practice. This is not a model of how to do things but a critical analogical move which may inspire and problematise. Such analogical 'seeing' is paralleled in Ruskin's own laying alongside each other the biblical text and his contemporary realities, which I have called in Chapter 5 his 'hermeneutic of immediacy' and which works by comparison and analogy.

We cannot find some place from which we gain a calm, detached view, or a place in which there is no pressure and no constriction. We can find places of partial refuge from the maelstrom in which some measure of self-understanding and reflectiveness are possible. Think of Ruskin writing his diaries in the midst of his existential crisis of faith, literally on the move through Europe with the very parents who were part of the cause of his crisis, studying Paul's letter to the Romans in the cracks of the day and writing notes in his diaries amid the notes on the places he visited and the rocks and plants he saw. Think of Giles Fraser reaching for an understanding of his own actions as he reaches for a borrowed razor, touching base in flashes of connection with the Bible over and over again as he tries to give some account of himself to a newspaper interviewer, in the midst of a rapidly moving situation which is being reported on the front pages of the national daily newspapers. Think of the leaders of the Palestinian Christians, writing out of 'this moment in history we are living through', where '[t]he hearts of the faithful are full of pain and questioning'. We write in the cracks of life, and this is the place from which we use our Bibles in public theology with meaning and power. Such positioning *in medias res* is not a hindrance, but is essential to significant 'seeing' of the situation and of the Bible. This is life on the margins and yet in the midst of things.

What We Bring with Us to the Bible – the (Auto)biographical

The lasting impression Giles Fraser's interview has made on me is the way his deeply treasured commitments determine his pattern of seeing and of practice in a crisis: 'It was catholic inner city worship and *for me it caught a particular aspect of what I believe*' (my italics). The whole interview is redolent not of making connections but of *seeing* connections.

Ruskin too is interested in the autobiographical.[4] This interest is specifically applied to his Bible reading, with constant scrutiny of his own reading history. More than that, his commitments and priorities, his likes and dislikes determine his interpretative moves: his commitment to justice and servanthood as heart of gospel, his dislike of exclusivity and arrogance, his suspicion of the obscure and other-worldly, his impatience with what is not useful in this life.

I cannot understand the practice of the Professional Doctorate programme without understanding my own commitments and my own questions. So my commitment to the significance of human experience for learning, and to human flourishing as the *telos*, the final purpose, of learning is central. My use of the Bible is determined by that, as much as it is determined by my personal history of engagement with the Bible in the contexts I have lived, and also by the explicit intellectual positions I have taken up in relation to biblical authority and interpretation. Most of all, my use of the Bible is fashioned by the emotional history I have with it, which is inextricable from my history of life and my relationships with others. From here comes my love and warmth towards it, and from here my ambiguity; from here my desire to stay, and my desire to escape.

With the autobiographical must come reflection on our own position, if we are to be at all critical. We need, like Ruskin, a consciousness of our own biblical reading history and, with that, a sense of its place in the wider public reading history and in reflective mapping of that reading history. This is what the discipline of biblical hermeneutics can give us. This book has in part been a conscious redressing of the balance towards the autobiographical, not as a means of evading criticism – far from it – but as a means of engaging a subjectivity that is more penetrating and comprehensive in its understanding than a supposedly detached, 'objective' view.

---

4   His autobiography *Praeterita* is one of his most wonderful works and a good place for the beginner to start.

An Inductive Approach

From the start the Professional Doctorate programme has positioned itself within a research methodology that is inductive, not deductive, and that is idiographic not nomothetic. That is to say, it has invited researchers to begin with the detailed particulars of their practice, in all their ambiguity and fragmentation, and to work to understand these better with a view to achieving better performances and practices, rather than to start from law-like principles and theories. We have understood *theological* reflection as one of the tools whereby more complete performances and practices might be achieved. 'More complete' does not necessarily signify 'more efficient, more cost effective', but the very values that might make a thing 'better' are themselves part of what is under scrutiny.

The commitment to inductive working, and to openness with regard to values, constitutes a challenge to some modes of doing theology and of using the Bible. John Swinton and Harriet Mowat in their immensely useful *Practical Theology and Qualitative Research* open up the question of 'areas of tensions and apparent contradiction, particularly over epistemology and the nature of truth and knowledge' between an inductive research approach and the traditional claims of theological truth.[5] They answer in terms of a critical faithfulness which is hospitable but which requires conversion: 'In our case this means qualitative research moving from a position which is fragmented and without a specific telos or goal, to a position where it is grafted in to God's redemptive intentions for the world.'[6]

It is precisely this position, or at least the strong version of it, that experience of the Professional Doctorate causes me to challenge. First, qualitative research itself is in fact normally done with a very specific intention in mind. Second, to exempt the theological understanding from the possibility of being radically questioned and shaped as a consequence of criticism seems to me to have only gone part of the way. We work with the unsystematic and fragmented, in a way that is not accountable to a predetermined model or methodology. In this we constantly work with ambiguity and the contested, as the borders of the sacred and the secular are broken down into a thousand 'minute particulars',[7] like Ruskin tolerating a high level of doubt and uncertainty and being interrogative of everything. It is in part the inability to work in this fragmented and contested way that we saw in Chapter 10 'flattened' the message of the Kairos Palestine document.

---

[5]   Swinton and Mowat, *Practical Theology*, p. 73.
[6]   Swinton and Mowat, *Practical Theology*, p. 92.
[7]   A wonderful expression used extensively by William Blake, for example in *Jerusalem* Chapter 3, plate 55, line 60, Blake, p.687. See p.82 footnote 4.

'Seeing' Connections not "Making' Connections

This critical interrogation of practices and of values, in which the world we live in and the traditions we are shaped by, the book of the Bible *as well as* the book of life, are set side by side, is not fundamentally a practice of *making* connections but of *seeing* connections. In practical theology, in the engagement of the Bible with the book of life, we need to pay less attention to the hunt for a transferable and generalisable model of making connections, and more attention to the discipline of seeing well those individual minute particulars that lie before us: critically, imaginatively and courageously, as well as analogically and comparatively.

And Finally ...

This book has taken me on a journey. I started out with a problem: what happens when we try to wrestle with life and the Bible? Orientated from the beginning in the 'readerly' quarter of the hermeneutical map, I have repeatedly explored the terrain of self-involvement, starting with Schleiermacher and pausing longer with Ruskin. My constant companions have been the dialectic between the book that is the Bible and the book of life as the foundation of practical, and thus public, theology; and John Ruskin, the reader of multiple texts, the seer with the eye and with the imagination. I have found the key to seeing not only clearly but prophetically, and above all with the heart, to be a subjectivity, driven by passion and attention to the world's woes. Such critical self-awareness and self-acceptance encourage a creative negotiation between the positive and the negative feelings, the constructive and the deconstructive analyses, the personal and the political. This allows space for critical friendship with the Bible. I have learnt that 'seeing' connections is more important than 'making' connections, that models and methods should not supplant inspiration and intuition, and reflection upon them, based on an informed 'seeing' of what is around us. Reality is more fluid, conflicted and plural than we sometimes try to maintain, and acceptance of this in ourselves encourages acceptance of it in one another. In all this I have found a hotline between myself and Ruskin.

Polarisation into two traditions of engaging the text of the Bible and the text of life, one of which is acceptance of the Bible as we have it and sits 'under the text' and eschews the 'tyranny of experience', the other of which is suspicious of the Bible in the light of experience of the Bible's effects and fears the 'tyranny of the text', is unhelpful. The reality is that commitments, visions and experiences in both traditions are much more fluid and mixed than that would suggest, and there are strategies we can share and on which we can build together. I have suggested three specific ways we can move forward: deeper attention to how our own stories and experiences engage with the Bible, and critical reflection on these; an acceptance of both love for and ambiguity towards the Bible within ourselves in the light of experience; and the welcoming of a more fragmented, sporadic, paradoxical and imaginative 'seeing' of connections and analogies rather than a mechanical adherence to models and methods in the 'making' of connections. Two of these are initially centred on the self. I make no apology for that; attention to the self that is both critical and accepting is an essential prerequisite for good attention to that which is other.

An Invitation

What do I hope that you the reader will take from this journey? Not a blueprint, not a method, not even really a map. Passion, inspiration, courage, some more tools with which to be critical. Most of all I hope the journey has awakened a desire to explore your own history and its possible relationship with the remarkable collection of texts that is the Bible, attention to the voices of our ancestors in the journey of life who have engaged in a similar task, and the relationship of all this to the flourishing of the human community of which you and I are a part.

From beginning to end this book has been about criticism, about the fact that 'for a human being the unexamined life is not worth living'. But the heart of practical theology, the very motor of its existence, is not an arid world of academic criticism, however impassioned and however just, but about life, for 'something living is dearer to me than all the treasure in the world'. We live in a world of conflict. It has ever been so, and human life, in all its richness, demands attention to 'The Other', whether human or divine. Blake understood that well, and encapsulated the fact that the threat to life is the easy resort to negation and destruction rather than the difficult path of understanding and negotiation between opposites. What is required is acceptance of the other, for 'Without contraries there is no progression'. The future of theology, practical theology included, involves that breadth of vision and the human embrace where one sees in the face of our neighbour the face of God: for 'There is no other light than this, by which they can see each other's faces and live.'[8]

---

[8]   Ruskin, *Works*, 17, 59.

Bibliography

Primary Sources

The Holy Bible, containing the Old and New Testaments: New Revised Standard Version, Anglicized Edition (Oxford: Oxford University Press, 1995).

Ruskin

Quotations from Ruskin's published works are taken from the Library Edition:
Cook, E.T. and A. Wedderburn (eds), *The Works of John Ruskin*, 39 vols (London: George Allen, 1903–12), referred to as *Works*, volume, page number.

British Library, Egerton 3046, Evangelistarium. Ruskin's annotations to Greek Gospel Lectionary.
Ruskin Library, Lancaster University, Ruskin Foundation, John Ruskin, Diaries for 1858/1859: RF MS 11, unpublished.
Ruskin Museum, Coniston, 'Sermon Notes on the Pentateuch' (from the third volume of a set of five booklets by John Ruskin), transcribed by Margaret Clunan, Documentation Assistant, Ruskin Museum.

Burd, V.A., *The Winnington Letters: John Ruskin's Correspondence with Margaret Alexis Bell and the Children at Winnington Hall* (Cambridge, Mass.: Belknap Press of Harvard University Press, 1969).
Dickinson, Rachel (ed.), *John Ruskin's Correspondence with Joan Severn: Sense and Nonsense Letters* (London: Modern Humanities Research Association and Maney Publishing, 2009).
Evans, Joan and John Howard Whitehouse (eds), *The Diaries of John Ruskin*, 3 vols (Oxford: Clarendon, 1956–59).
Ruskin, John, *Praeterita*, ed. Francis O'Gorman (Oxford: Oxford University Press, 2012).

Other Primary Sources

Blake, W., *Blake: Complete Writings*, ed. G. Keynes (Oxford: Oxford University Press, 1966).
Calvin, John, *Institutes of the Christian Religion*, ed. John T. McNeill, Library of Christian Classics 20, 21 (London: SCM Press, 1961).
Cohen, Leonard, 'The Future', in *Stranger Music: Selected Poems and Songs* (London: Jonathan Cape, 1993), p. 370.

Eliot, T.S., *Collected Poems 1909–1962* (London: Faber and Faber, 1963).

Kairos document, *Challenge to the Church: A Theological Comment on the Political Crisis in South Africa: The Kairos Document* (London: Catholic Institute for International Relations, 1985).

de Vigny, Alfred, *Möise*, in *The Oxford Book of French Verse XIIIth–XIXth Century*, chosen by St John Lucas (Oxford: Clarendon Press, 1907).

WCC, *Living Letters: A Report of Visits to the Churches during the Ecumenical Decade – Churches in Solidarity with Women* (Geneva: WCC, 1997).

Secondary Sources

Anderson, Herbert and Edward Foley, *Mighty Stories, Dangerous Rituals: Weaving Together the Human and the Divine* (San Francisco: Jossey-Bass, 2001).

Ballard, Paul, 'The Use of Scripture', in Bonnie J. Miller-McLemore (ed.), *The Wiley-Blackwell Companion to Practical Theology* (Oxford: Wiley-Blackwell, 2011), pp. 163–72.

Ballard, Paul and Stephen Holmes (eds), *The Bible in Pastoral Practice: Readings in the Place and Function of Scripture in the Church* (Grand Rapids, Mich.: Eerdmans, 2006).

Ballard, Paul and John Pritchard, *Practical Theology in Action*, 2nd edn (London: SPCK, 2006).

Barth, Karl, *Church Dogmatics IV, The Doctrine of Reconciliation*, trans. G.W. Bromiley (Edinburgh: T&T Clark, 1956).

Barth, Karl, 'The Preface to the Second Edition', *The Epistle to the Romans*, trans. Edwyn Hoskyns (Oxford: Oxford University Press, 1968; first published 1933).

Barth, Karl, *The Word of God and the Word of Man*, trans. Douglas Horton (London: Hodder & Stoughton, 1928).

Karl Barth-Rudolf Bultmann Letters 1922–1966, ed. Bernd Jaspert, trans. and ed. Geoffrey W. Bromiley (Edinburgh: T&T Clark, 1982).

Bartholomew, Craig, Colin Greene and Karl Möller, *Renewing Biblical Interpretation* (Carlisle: Paternoster, 2000).

Barton, John, 'Classifying Biblical Criticism', *Journal for the Study of the Old Testament*, 29 (1984): 19–35.

Bennett, Zoë, '"There is no other light than this by which they can see one another's faces and live": John Ruskin and the Bible', in Neil Messer and Angus Paddison (eds), *The Bible: Culture, Community and Society* (Edinburgh: T&T Clark International, in press)

Bennett, Zoë, 'Creation made Image and Image Made Word: John Ruskin on JMW Turner's "Snow Storm"', in D. Pezzoli-Olgiati and C. Rowland (eds), *Approaches to Visuality in Religion*, Research in Contemporary Religion (Göttingen: Vandenhoeck und Ruprecht, 2011), pp. 249–60.

Bennett, Zoë, 'Ruskin, the Bible and the Death of Rose La Touche: A "torn manuscript of the human soul"', in Michael Lieb, Emma Mason, Jonathan Roberts and Christopher Rowland (eds), *The Oxford Handbook of Reception History of the Bible* (Oxford: Oxford University Press, 2011), pp. 576–89.

Bennett, Zoë, '"To see fearlessly, pitifully": What Does John Ruskin Have to Offer to Practical Theology?', *International Journal of Practical Theology*, 14.2 (2011): 189–203.

Bennett, Zoë, '"A fact full of power or a dream full of meaning": The Influence of Religion and the Bible on Ruskin's Social, Political and Economic Critique', *Ruskin Review and Bulletin*, 6.2 (Autumn 2010): 35–47.

Bennett, Zoë, '"By Fors, thus blotted with a double cross": Some Notes upon the Death of Rose La Touche', *Ruskin Review and Bulletin*, 5.2 (Autumn 2009): 27–34.

Bennett, Zoë, 'Theology and the Researching Professional: The Professional Doctorate in Practical Theology', *Theology*, CXII.869 (2009): 333–43.

Bennett, Zoë, '"To be taught to see is to gain word and thought at once": John Ruskin and Practical Theology', *Practical Theology*, 1.1 (2008): 85–93.

Bennett, Zoë, 'Evaluating the Feasibility of a Cross-Institutional Professional Doctorate in Practical Theology: Project Report', *Discourse*, 6.2 (2007): 55–77.

Bennett, Zoë, '"Action is the life of All": The Praxis-based Epistemology of Liberation Theology', in Christopher Rowland (ed.), *The Cambridge Companion to Liberation Theology*, 2nd edn (Cambridge: Cambridge University Press, 2007), pp. 39–54.

Bennett, Zoë, *Incorrigible Plurality: Teaching Pastoral Theology in an Ecumenical Context*, Contact Pastoral Monograph 14 (Edinburgh: Contact Pastoral Trust, 2004).

Bennett, Zoë, Lucia Faltin and Melanie Wright, 'Critical Thinking and International Postgraduate Students', *Discourse*, 3.1 (2003): 63–94.

Bennett, Zoë and David Gowler (eds), *Radical Christian Voices and Practice: Essays in Honour of Christopher Rowland* (Oxford: Oxford University Press, 2012).

Bennett, Zoë and Elaine Graham, 'The Professional Doctorate in Practical Theology: Developing the Researching Professional in Practical Theology in Higher Education', *Journal of Adult Theological Education*, 5.1 (2008): 33–51.

Bennett, Zoë and Christopher Rowland, 'Contextual and Advocacy Readings of the Bible', in Paul Ballard and Stephen Holmes (eds), *The Bible in Pastoral Practice: Readings in the Place and Function of Scripture in the Church* (Grand Rapids, Mich.: Eerdmans, 2006), pp. 174–90.

Bennett Moore, Zoë, 'Pastoral Theology as Hermeneutics', *British Journal of Theological Education*, 12.1 (2001): 7–18.

Boff, Clodovis, *Theology and Praxis: Epistemological Foundations* (Maryknoll, NY: Orbis, 1987).

Boff, Leonardo and Clodovis Boff, *Introducing Liberation Theology*, trans. Paul Burns (Maryknoll, NY: Orbis, 1987).

Bridges-Johns, Cheryl, *Pentecostal Formation: A Pedagogy among the Oppressed*, *Journal of Pentecostal Theology* Supplement Series 2 (Sheffield: Sheffield Academic Press, 1993).

Brown, Sally, 'Hermeneutical Theory', in Bonnie J. Miller-McLemore (ed.), *The Wiley-Blackwell Companion to Practical Theology* (Oxford: Wiley-Blackwell, 2011), pp. 112–22.

Brunhes, H.J., *Ruskin et la Bible* (Paris: Perrin, 1901).

Bultmann, Rudolf, 'Is Exegesis Without Presuppositions Possible?', in *Existence and Faith: Shorter Writings of Rudolf Bultmann*, trans. Schubert M. Ogden (Cleveland, OH: World Publishing, 1960), pp. 342–52; reprinted in K. Mueller-Vollmer (ed.), *The Hermeneutics Reader* (New York: Continuum, 1985), pp. 242–7.

Busch, Eberhard, *Karl Barth: His Life from Letters and Autobiographical Texts*, trans. John Bowden (London: SCM Press, 1976).

Cameron, Helen, John Reader and Victoria Slater with Christopher Rowland, *Theological Reflection for Human Flourishing* (London: SCM Press, 2012).

Capps, Donald, *Pastoral Care and Hermeneutics* (Philadelphia: Fortress Press, 1984).

Collingwood, W.G., *The Ruskin Cross at Coniston* (Ulverston: W. Holmes, 1910; reprinted Coniston: M.J. Salts, January 2000).

Collingwood, W.G., *Ruskin's Relics* (London: Isbister, 1903).

Corns, T.N., A. Hughes and D. Loewenstein (eds), *The Complete Works of Gerrard Winstanley*, 2 vols (Oxford: Oxford University Press, 2009).

Davidson, Donald, 'What Metaphors Mean', in *Inquiries into Truth and Interpretation* (Oxford: Oxford University Press, 1984), pp. 245–64.

Davies, W.D., *The Gospel and the Land: Early Christianity and Jewish Territorial Doctrine* (Sheffield: JSOT Press, 1994).

Drury, John, 'Ruskin's Way: *tout a fait comme un oiseau*', in S. Collini, R. Whitmore and B. Young (eds), *History, Religion, and Culture: British Intellectual History, 1750–1950* (Cambridge: Cambridge University Press, 2000), pp. 156–76.

Eagles, Stuart, *After Ruskin: The Social and Political Legacies of a Victorian Prophet 1870–1920*, Oxford Historical Monographs (Oxford: Oxford University Press, 2011).

Edwards, David L. with John Stott, *Essentials: A Liberal-Evangelical Dialogue* (London: Hodder & Stoughton, 1988).

Farley, Edward, 'Interpreting Situations: An Inquiry into the Nature of Practical Theology', in James Woodward and Stephen Pattison (eds), *The Blackwell Reader in Pastoral and Practical Theology* (Oxford: Blackwell, 2000), pp. 135–45.

Farley, Edward, *Theologia: The Fragmentation and Unity of Theological Education* (Philadelphia: Fortress Press, 1983).

Farley, Edward and Peter Hodgson, 'Scripture and Tradition', in Peter Hodgson and Robert King (eds), *Christian Theology: An Introduction to its Traditions and Tasks* (London: SPCK, 1982), pp. 35–61.

Fontaine, Carole R., 'The Abusive Bible: On the Use of Feminist Methods in Pastoral Contexts', in Athalya Brenner and Carole R. Fontaine (eds), *A Feminist Companion to Reading the Bible: Approaches, Methods and Strategies* (Sheffield: Sheffield Academic Press, 1997), pp. 84–113.

Frei, Hans, *The Eclipse of Biblical Narrative: A Study in Eighteenth and Nineteenth Century Hermenuetics* (New Haven and London: Yale University Press, 1974).

Gadamer, Hans-Georg, 'The Historicity of Understanding', in Kurt Mueller-Vollmer (ed.), *The Hermeneutics Reader: Texts of the German Tradition from the Enlightenment to the Present* (New York: Continuum, 1985), pp. 256–74.

Gerkin, Charles V., *An Introduction to Pastoral Care* (Nashville: Abingdon Press, 1997).

Gibbs, M. and E. (arr.), *The Bible References in the Works of John Ruskin* (London: George Allen, 1898).

Graham, Elaine L., 'The Professional Doctorate in Practical Theology: An Idea Whose Time has Come?', *International Journal of Practical Theology*, 10.2 (March 2007): 298–311.

Graham, Elaine L., *Transforming Practice: Pastoral Theology in an Age of Uncertainty*, (London: Mowbray, 1996; reprinted and reissued Eugene, Ore.: Wipf and Stock, 2002).

Gutiérrez, Gustavo, 'The Task and Content of Liberation Theology', in Christopher Rowland (ed.), *The Cambridge Companion to Liberation Theology* (Cambridge: Cambridge University Press, 1999), pp. 25–32.

Hampson, Daphne, *Theology and Feminism* (Oxford: Basil Blackwell, 1990).

Hegel, G.W.F., *Lectures on the Philosophy of Religion of 1824*, Vol.1: *Introduction and the Concept of Religion*, ed. P.C. Hodgson, trans. R.F. Brown (Berkeley: University of California Press, 1984).

Hewison, Robert, *John Ruskin: The Argument of the Eye* (London: Thames & Hudson, 1976).

Hewison, Robert, *Ruskin on Venice* (New Haven and London: Yale University Press, 2009).

Hilton, Tim, *John Ruskin* (New Haven and London: Yale University Press, 2002).

Holgate, David A. and Rachel Starr, *SCM Study Guide to Biblical Hermeneutics* (London: SCM Press, 2006).

Kant, Immanuel, *Critique of Pure Reason*, trans. Norman Kemp Smith, 2nd edn (London: Macmillan, 1933).

Käsemann, Ernst, *Commentary on Romans*, trans. and ed. G.W. Bromiley (London: SCM Press, 1980).

Kelsey, David H., *The Uses of Scripture in Recent Theology* (London: SCM Press, 1975).

Klemm, David E. 'Culture, Arts, and Religion', in Jacqueline Mariña (ed.), *The Cambridge Companion to Friedrich Schleiermacher* (Cambridge: Cambridge University Press, 2005), pp. 251–68.

Kolb, David, *Experiential Learning: Experience as the Source of Learning and Development* (Englewood Cliffs, NJ: Prentice Hall, 1984).

Landow, George, *Victorian Types, Victorian Shadows* (Boston, London and Henley: Routledge & Kegan Paul, 1980).

Lash, Nicholas, *Easter in Ordinary: Reflections on Human Experience and the Knowledge of God* (London: SCM Press, 1988).

Lash, Nicholas, 'Performing the Scriptures', in *Theology on the Way to Emmaus* (London: SCM Press, 1986), pp. 37–46.

Law, Jeremy, 'Theological Imagination and Human Flourishing', in Mike Higton, Jeremy Law and Christopher Rowland (eds), *Theology and Human Flourishing: Essays in Honor of Timothy J. Gorringe* (Eugene, Ore.: Wipf and Stock, 2011).

Leach, Jane, 'Pastoral Theology as Attention', *Contact. Practical Theology and Pastoral Care*, 153 (2007): 19–32.

Lyall, David, *Integrity of Pastoral Care* (London: SPCK, 2001).

MacGregor, Neil, *The History of the World in 100 Objects* (London: Penguin, 2012).

Masalha, Nur, *The Bible and Zionism: Invented Traditions, Archaeology and Post-Colonialism in Israel-Palestine* (London and New York: Zed Books, 2007).

Miller-McLemore, Bonnie J., 'The "Clerical Paradigm": A Fallacy of Misplaced Concreteness?', *International Journal of Practical Theology*, 11 (2007): 19–38.

Miller-McLemore, Bonnie J., 'The Living Human Web: Pastoral Theology at the Turn of the Century', in Jeanne Stevenson Moessner (ed.), *Through the Eyes of Women: Insights for Pastoral Care* (Minneapolis: Fortress Press 1996), pp. 9–26.

Miller-McLemore, Bonnie J. (ed.), *The Wiley-Blackwell Companion to Practical Theology* (Oxford: Wiley-Blackwell, 2011).

Moltmann, Jürgen, *Theology of Hope: On the Ground and the Implications for a Christian Eschatology* (London: SCM Press, 2002; first published in German, 1965).

Morgan, Robert, '*Sachkritik* in Reception History', *Journal for the Study of the New Testament*, 33 (December 2010): 175–90.

Mosala, Itumeleng J., *Biblical Hermeneutics and Black Theology in South Africa* (Grand Rapids, Mich.: W.B. Eerdmans, 1989).

Mueller-Vollmer, Kurt (ed.), *The Hermeneutics Reader: Texts of the German Tradition from the Enlightenment to the Present* (New York: Continuum, 1985).

Oeming, Manfred, *Contemporary Biblical Hermeneutics: An Introduction*, trans. Joachim F. Vette (Aldershot: Ashgate, 2006).

Pattison, Stephen, *A Critique of Pastoral Care*, 3rd edn (London: SCM Press, 2000).

Pembroke, Neil, *Renewing Pastoral Practice: Trinitarian Perspectives on Pastoral Care and Counselling* (Aldershot: Ashgate, 2006).

Penny, Nicholas, *Ruskin's Drawings* (Oxford: Ashmolean Museum, 2004).

Petrella, Ivan, 'The Futures of Liberation Theology', in Zoë Bennett and David Gowler (eds), *Radical Christian Voices and Practice: Essays in Honour of Christopher Rowland* (Oxford: Oxford University Press, 2012), pp. 201–10.

Reif, Stefan, 'The Jewish Contribution to Biblical Interpretation', in John Barton (ed.), *The Cambridge Companion to Biblical Interpretation* (Cambridge: Cambridge University Press, 1998), pp. 143–59.

Renan, Ernest, *Souvenirs d'Enfance et de Jeunesse* (Paris: Editions Gallimard, 1983).

Robinson, John, *Wrestling with Romans* (London: SCM Press, 1979).

Rowland, Christopher, *Blake and the Bible* (New Haven: Yale University Press, 2011).

Rowland, Christopher (ed.), *The Cambridge Companion to Liberation Theology* (Cambridge: Cambridge University Press, 1999; 2nd edn, 2007).

Rowland, Christopher, '"I have Writ, I have Acted, I have Peace"', in Zoë Bennett and David Gowler (eds), *Radical Christian Voices and Practice: Essays in Honour of Christopher Rowland* (Oxford: Oxford University Press, 2012), pp. 257–74.

Rowland, Christopher, 'The "Interested" Interpreter', in R. Carroll, M. Daniel, David J.A. Clines and Philip R. Davies (eds), *The Bible in Human Society: Essays in Honour of John Rogerson*, Journal for the Study of the Old Testament Supplement Series 200 (Sheffield: Sheffield Academic Press, 1995), pp. 429–44.

Rowland, Christopher, *The Open Heaven: A Study of Apocalyptic in Judaism and Early Christianity* (London: SPCK, 1982).

Rowland, Christopher and Zoë Bennett, '"Action is the Life of All": New Testament Theology and Practical Theology', in C. Rowland and C. Tuckett (eds), *The Nature of New Testament Theology* (Oxford: Blackwell, 2006), pp. 186–206.

Rowland, Christopher and Mark Corner, *Liberating Exegesis: The Challenge of Liberation Theology to Biblical Studies* (London: SPCK, 1989).

Rowland, Christopher and John Roberts, *The Bible for Sinners: Interpretation in the Present Time* (London: SPCK, 2008).

Ruether, Rosemary Radford, *Faith and Fratricide: The Theological Roots of Anti-Semitism* (Eugene, Ore.: Wipf and Stock, 1974).

Ruether, Rosemary Radford, *Sexism and God-talk: Towards a Feminist Theology* (London: SCM, 2002; originally published 1983).

Sardar, Ziauddin, *Reading the Qur'an* (London: Hurst, 2011).

Schleiermacher, Friedrich, *Brief Outline of Theology as a Field of Study*, translation of the 1811 and 1830 editions, with essays and notes, by Terrence N. Tice (Lewiston, NY: E. Mellen Press, 1990).

Schleiermacher, Friedrich, *The Christian Faith*, trans. M.R. Mackintosh and J.S. Stewart (Edinburgh: T&T Clark, 1928).

Schleiermacher, Friedrich, *On the Glaubenslehre: Two Letters to Dr Lücke*, trans. James Duke and Francis Fiorenza (Chico, Calif.: Scholars Press, 1981).

Schleiermacher, Friedrich, *Hermeneutics: The Handwritten Manuscripts*, ed. H. Kimmerle, trans. J. Duke and J. Forstman (Missoula, Mont.: Scholars Press, 1977).

Schleiermacher, Friedrich, *On Religion: Speeches to its Cultured Despisers*, trans. Richard Coulter (Cambridge: Cambridge University Press 1988; first published 1799).

Schön, Donald, *The Reflective Practitioner: How Professionals Think in Action* (Aldershot: Ashgate, 2003; originally published London: Maurice Temple Smith, 1983).

Schweitzer, Albert, *The Quest of the Historical Jesus: A Critical Study of its Progress from Reimarus to Wrede*, with a preface by F.C. Burkitt, 2nd English edn, trans. W. Montgomery (London: A & C Black, 1911).

Shipani, Daniel S., 'Case Study Method', in Bonnie J. Miller-McLemore (ed.), *The Wiley-Blackwell Companion to Practical Theology* (Oxford: Wiley-Blackwell, 2011), pp. 91–101.

Soskice, Janet Martin, 'Love and Attention', in *The Kindness of God* (Oxford: Oxford University Press, 2007), pp. 7–34.

Soskice, Janet Martin, 'The Truth looks Different from Here or on Seeking the Unity of Truth from a Diversity of Perspectives', in H. Regan and A. Torrance (eds), *Christ and Context: The Confrontation between Gospel and Culture* (Edinburgh: T&T Clark, 1993), pp. 43–59.

Spear, Jeffrey L., 'Ruskin as a Prejudiced Reader', *English Literary History*, 49 (1982): 73–98.

Storrar, Will, '2007: A Kairos Moment for Public Theology', *International Journal of Public Theology*, 1.1 (2007): 5–25.

Sweeney, James, Gemma Simmonds and David Lonsdale (eds), *Keeping Faith in Practice: Aspects of Catholic Pastoral Theology* (London: SCM Press, 2010).

Swinton, John and Harriet Mowat, *Practical Theology and Qualitative Research* (London: SCM Press, 2006).

Thiselton, Anthony, *New Horizons in Hermeneutics: The Theory and Practice of Transforming Bible Reading*, 20th Anniversary Edition (Grand Rapids, Michigan: Zondervan, 2012).

Thiselton, Anthony, *The Two Horizons: New Testament Hermeneutics and philosophical Description with Special Reference to Heidegger, Bultmann, Gadamer, and Wittgenstein* (Grand Rapids, Mich.: Eerdmans; Exeter: Paternoster, 1980).

Tilley, Maureen A., *The Bible in Christian North Africa: The Donatist World* (Minneapolis: Augsburg Fortress, 1997).

Tracy, David, *The Analogical Imagination: Christian Theology and the Culture of Pluralism* (New York: Crossroad, 1981).

Trible, Phyllis, *Texts of Terror: Literary-feminist Readings of Biblical Narratives* (Philadelphia: Fortress Press, 1984).

Tyndale, Wendy R., *Protestants in Communist East Germany: In the Storm of the World* (Aldershot: Ashgate, 2010).

Tyrrell, George, *Christianity at the Crossroads* (London: Longmans, Green, 1910).

Van Til, Cornelius, Introduction to B.B. Warfield, *The Inspiration and Authority of the Bible*, ed. Samuel G. Craig (Philadelphia: Presbyterian and Reformed Publishing, 1948).

Village, Andrew, *The Bible and Lay People: An Empirical Approach to Ordinary Hermeneutics* (Aldershot: Ashgate, 2007).

Walton, Roger, 'Using the Bible and Christian Tradition in Theological Reflection', *British Journal of Theological Education*, 13.2 (January 2003): 133–51.

Warfield, B.B., *The Inspiration and Authority of the Bible*, ed. Samuel G. Craig (Philadelphia: Presbyterian and Reformed Publishing, 1948).

Wheeler, Michael, *Ruskin's God* (Cambridge: Cambridge University Press, 1999).

Wright, Tom, 'How Can the Bible be Authoritative?', *Vox Evangelica*, 21 (1991): 7–32.

Newspapers

Glancey, Jonathan, 'Of Skeletons and Souls', *The Guardian*, 19 June 2009, p. 35.

Rusbridger, Alan, 'A Troublesome Priest? I Get Fitted Up as Wat Tyler, But I'm No Radical', interview with Rev Dr Giles Fraser, *The Guardian*, Friday, 28 October 2011, pp. 16–17.

Websites

http://www.anglicancommunion.org/listening/ (accessed 31.07.2012).

http://www.brantwood.org.uk/ (accessed 24.07.2012).

http://www.bridgemanart.com/ (accessed 09.08.2012).

http://www9.georgetown.edu/faculty/jod/texts/moralia1.html (accessed 26.07.2012).

http://www.guildofstgeorge.org.uk (accessed 25.07.2012).

http://www.kairospalestine.ps/sites/default/Documents/English.pdf (accessed 02.11.11).

http://www.lancs.ac.uk/fass/ruskin/empi/3rdedition/3b374.htm (accessed 27.07.2012).

http://www.lancs.ac.uk/users/ruskinlib/ (accessed 23.07.2012).

http://www.metrolyrics.com/that-dont-make-it-junk-lyrics-leonard-cohen.html (accessed 25.07.2012).

http://www.nalanda.nitc.ac.in/resources/english/etext-project/biography/gandhi/part4.chapter18.html (accessed 25.07.2012).

http://occupylsx.org/ (accessed 07.11.11).

http://rmt.org/our_vision_and_values (accessed 30.04.12).

http://ruskin.ashmolean.org/ (accessed 26.01.2012).

http://www.stpaulsinstitute.org.uk/Mission (accessed 14.11.11).

http://www.tate.org.uk/art/artworks/turner-snow-storm-steam-boat-off-a-harbours-mouth-n00530 (accessed 27.07.2012).

http://www.vatican.va/archive/hist_councils/ii_vatican_council/documents/vat-ii_const_19651207_gaudium-et-spes_en.html (accessed 31.07.12).

http://www.victorianweb.org/authors/ruskin/index.html (accessed 23.07.2012).

Index

Biblical References

Genesis (61)
Gen. 30.7–8 (9)
Gen. 32.24–6 (9)
Exodus 3 (123)
2 Kings 6.17 (99)
Isaiah (75)
Isaiah 55.11 (100)
Ezekiel (75, 99)
Amos 5.10–15 (99)
Amos 7.7–9 (99)
Amos 7.14–15 (99)
Matt. 5.3 (67)
Matt. 25.40 (96)
Matt. 27 (73)
Mark (68)
Luke 17.21 (122)
Luke 22. 24–7 (68)
John 11 (75)
John 18.36 (122)
Acts 15 (19)
Romans (19, 29–30, 55, 67, 68, 70, 104–5, 122–3, 131)
Rom. 1.5 (70, 104)
Rom. 8 (122)

Rom. 14.17 (123)
Romans 9–11 (19)
Corinthians (20)
1 Cor. 2.9–16 (29)
1 Cor. 2.11–12 (97)
1 Cor. 3.16 (97)
2 Cor. 3.17–18 (29)
1 Cor. 6.19 (97)
1 Cor. 10 (48)
1 Cor. 10.1–4 (77)
1 Cor. 10.1–13 (18)
1 Corinthians 13 (122)
Gal. 1.4 (104)
Galatians 3 (124)
Gal. 3.28 (44)
Gal. 6.16 (123)
Colossians (30)
Hebrews (123)
Heb. 1.1–2 (20, 123)
Heb. 10 (71)
1 Peter (13, 75)
Revelation (61, 99)
Rev. 22.14–17 (67)